T0381465

RESCUING ME:

When you can no longer not be you
& being willing to take the inner journey,
revisiting the pains to claim the gains.

PAULA A. BRAVO

BALBOA.PRESS
A DIVISION OF HAY HOUSE

Balboa Press books may be ordered through booksellers or by contacting:

Balboa Press
A Division of Hay House
1663 Liberty Drive
Bloomington, IN 47403
www.balboapress.com
844-682-1282

Because of the dynamic nature of the Internet, any web addresses or links contained in this book may have changed since publication and may no longer be valid. The views expressed in this work are solely those of the author and do not necessarily reflect the views of the publisher, and the publisher hereby disclaims any responsibility for them.

The author of this book does not dispense medical advice or prescribe the use of any technique as a form of treatment for physical, emotional, or medical problems without the advice of a physician, either directly or indirectly. The intent of the author is only to offer information of a general nature to help you in your quest for emotional and spiritual well-being. In the event you use any of the information in this book for yourself, which is your constitutional right, the author and the publisher assume no responsibility for your actions.

Any people depicted in stock imagery provided by Getty Images are models, and such images are being used for illustrative purposes only. Certain stock imagery © Getty Images.

Print information available on the last page.

ISBN: 979-8-7652-5879-8 (sc)
ISBN: 979-8-7652-5878-1 (e)

Library of Congress Control Number: 2024926852

Balboa Press rev. date: 01/13/2025

Contents

Introduction

"Hey. I was just wondering—what about me? Can I have a say in the way this life that's supposed to be my own will go?" If you've ever felt like your life is stuck on autopilot, too, and not in a good way, you might ask yourself the same.

I always told my two children, "When you lie in your bed at night, you are left to answer to you. So, take care of that first. Be nice about it. Do what makes you happy. Don't do anything just to make me happy; don't sacrifice your own happiness for mine. Your being happy will add to my happiness. This way we both win."

From this way of seeing life now—this way of living my own life—it actually feels good. It has a freeing essence to it. Learning to answer to myself soothed me and taught me a lot along the way.

It feels good to have positive talks throughout the day and before falling asleep. It feels nice to be nice to me; that still small voice I've found inside has been so caring. Every second, really, it is just me. So why has my relationship with myself felt so distant at times? Perhaps because I was so busy looking elsewhere. Why had I not asked that question before what about me? The first time I did my body felt the "newness" of it. I made room for it.

From the minute I asked myself that simple question, I was opened. I began to feel that misery could serve as the impetus for change, and the doors of mine were now swung open. What I had shared with my two children, that way of thinking took on a life of its own within me, too. It was multifaceted. A true Pandora's Box.

Answering myself, with honesty, became the new platform. I owed it to myself to step onto it and understand. I would lie in bed at night with my thoughts and do my best to shape them into something gentler than what they had ever been before. Being more careful in what I thought felt good, like something loving was going on—like something in the very air was changing. It felt natural and right for me. I wanted to keep going. I felt I had no choice— but in a good way. Like a performer choosing to be shot out of a cannon, there was excitement in my bones.

Life kept moving on as it does, and I had cleared a bit of room inside my mind for relief from all that had settled into place before. I began to like myself more each day. Yet there was a historical record of me that had been written already and it had some kind of kung fu master grip on me. I could feel that shit. And only I could do something about it. I needed some new tools to chisel down to the real me. Curiosity was sparked.

What did I see? Not out here in the physical world, but in my mind's eye? What reels were continually running and replaying? Well, this is where it got interesting, there was so much of me that wanted to be known. It was the me that existed underneath all the images others held of me—even the ones I had created, as well. The road to self-discovery, as we say, is a uniquely built one. And the driving force, a strong and steady one, is fueled by each of us. It comes in the form of self-love.

Think about the incredible power of a statement you can truly buy into. A statement that comes to your mind and gut and heart as innocently as a child enters the world. I am worthy of a good life, of course I am. Tending to the innocence of such a statement produces fruit sweeter than you have ever seen or tasted. Can you imagine? All of this growth happening inside of you, bearing fruit just for you.

Where you are led will fascinate you. And where that special moment occurs, a beautiful mystery full of enchantment awaits you. It can be a simple daily act that bursts open the floodgates of your soul. The element of surprise will be sure to delight you. That time you take to care enough to answer to yourself is an investment worth making—a seed worth dropping into the soil of your future.

When I leaned into these feelings toward myself, I finally got that "life makes sense" feeling. I have made so many changes to how I think. I really enjoy checking myself. I feel the drive in me to live—and to live in an honest way, treating myself kindly every single day.

The bread-crumb trail. Little by little, easy does it, enjoy the ride. That's what I kept hearing in my head. Always makes me smile.

I remember picking up books at thrift stores that I was just drawn to. They were all unique in explaining life. They talked about the mind and how powerful it is. Others talked about God or the Creator. They all aimed to impart some knowledge to the reader. I was intrigued by them. I'd never looked at life from these new perspectives. They shared truths I could feel in my gut. They felt like truth–like a lie was being exposed. Every time I went to a thrift store, there were more books that added to my eagerness to learn, to apply new shit to my life. I found concepts that made sense intellectually; they carried freedom within them.

All the new information I was reading and pondering fueled my eagerness to get to know myself better. I don't think I was fully aware it was taking place. And I wasn't convinced that I loved myself as much as I said I did. It felt like something was off, like a part of me was searching. I knew it was time to be real with myself and ask the tough questions. The call to know myself better was very strong and when I threw my hands in the air for the last time, it was with a smile and an open heart. I was excited about this challenge.

I wasn't going within myself to criticize or beat myself up; certain experiences had already done that. I wanted to comprehend why they happened. I wanted to see what it was that I set into motion or invited into my life. With no specific direction you know, or step-by-step system, I was moving differently through life. The difference was that I felt happy more often. I could tell I cared about myself. I always wanted to share my "aha moments" with my wife (at the time my girlfriend)–and with my kids, who usually called me weird. From time to time I'd be super excited about a lightbulb moment that'd I'd even share it with a coworker. All of it was fun. It still is. Lightbulb moments never get old.

All the ways life has led me to this level of happiness and peace began with me. Caring deeply about existing is beautiful. Ease comes over you. This ease is worth talking about. I thank those authors who shared their message, those who were open valves of expression. I am forever thankful for answering me in the most honest of ways, and for helping me know that love for myself is the foundation and springboard. I'm thankful that when the time came to know myself, self-love had been behind the scenes all along.

Self-love, what a beautiful thing. With it as my ever-present companion, I discovered all of me. I gathered myself. From those nights when I wanted to avoid the noise in my head to the nights when I eagerly awaited my alone time seems like a huge leap. But in all truth, it wasn't a leap at all. Instead, it was a bridge that led me to feel happy and free. The bridge from me to me is me. Now with all of me here, present and eager to keep moving, I share with you that it's time to walk in your rightful place. As you lie in your bed at night, be nice to that voice you hear inside. After all, it is really you.

"To live happily is an inward power of the soul."
—Marcus Aurelius, Meditations

THE SUBTLY OF CALLING
OUT TO YOURSELF

CHAPTER 1

Listen up, you *are* that important.

"Make the most of yourself...for
that is all there is of you."
–Ralph Waldo Emerson

"The only service you can render God is to give
expression to what he is trying to give the world,
through you. The only service you can render to God
is to make the very most of yourself in order that God
may live in you to the utmost of your possibilities."
–Wallace D. Wattles, The Science of Getting Rich

A voice within me whispered, "Let yourself think
differently. Only you know what you are doing inside
yourself, so fuck it if it's weird. Go about it from a new
angle. Change seats, go to another view, do what you
gotta' do to find you." Whoa, where did that thought
come from? I wondered if it was from the Janis Joplin
documentary I was watching on PBS. I had heard of
Janis Joplin and a few of her songs, but I didn't know
much about her or her career. I was in the middle of

folding laundry in my bedroom when I heard her singing on tv. Her voice drew me in. It was a bit raspy with lots of conviction about it. I decided to take the laundry folding to the room so I can hear more of her voice and get to know more about her. The words I heard next would cascade over my body and leave a lasting impression:

"To be true to myself, to be the person that was on the inside of me, and not play games. That's what I'm trying to do mostly in the whole world, is not bullshit myself and not bullshit anyone else."
–Janis Joplin

Fuck that was the best thing I had heard in what I thought was forever. It was so simple, so impactful, so true to what I was feeling I wanted, but not what I was living. I kept hitting the rewind button on my tv remote control, so that I could hear her say those words again. I was so desirous of hearing words that soothed my soul, and her words did just that for those couple of hours. The soothing would conjure up ideas that I did not want to admit to myself. I was a bullshitter, to myself and to others, ouch! Wearing that crown didn't sit well with me. The person inside, where is she? Have I ever met her, I asked myself. You know the one inside? Oh yeah, the girl that I keep hidden, that *her*.

The very next morning as I was lying in bed, I slowly opened my eyes and caught the sounds of birds singing outside my bedroom window; easy way to make me smile. I felt a cool breeze brush my face, it was refreshing and telling of a new morning. The bed felt safe and the sheets so cozy. I could feel myself drifting in and out of sleep. For as good as that moment felt, another feeling creeped in too, it was sadness. Not the kind that leads to shedding tears, but a sadness that felt like it'd been with me for many years. I was present to the comfort of my body in bed and the joy that the birds singing made me feel. So, I felt a bit confused as to how these two emotions could be happening at once. How could I be feeling so good, yet not fully enjoy it? Was I happy? Was I living the life I wanted to live? Was I making the most of myself, of my life? Good questions popped into my mind. Questions I wanted to answer. Then before my mind flashed the words 'know thyself'. And all I could think back to was Janis Joplin and me not wanting to be a bullshitter anymore either.

I may not know what is in your heart at this very moment, what emotion you are sensing within yourself, but what I do know is that understanding yourself is priceless; it's life giving to itself. As the Greeks said, "Know thyself", so that you may play a new role in the game of life—one of your choosing. Janis Joplin said she didn't want to play any games. I assume she didn't want to play around with her existence and sought to be as true to her being as possible. I was seeking to do the same, but I also wanted to add my own fun element to her inspiring words. This would be one of the ways I'd get better acquainted with the girl within, adding my own plot twists and having fun along the way.

The maxim "Know Thyself" was inscribed near the entrance to the temple of Apollo at Delphi. A maxim, a general truth or fundamental principle. Socrates elaborated on this concept and claimed to be wise only in knowing that he was ignorant. Isn't that where we start? We start living in ignorance and then it doesn't feel like living but more like surviving. To survive is to continue to exist. To live is to have life, to be full of vigor. And then we move to thriving, which is where we desire to be. To thrive is to prosper or flourish (Merriam-Webster).

I've come to understand that I was surviving every day. I existed here on Earth, attempting to make sense of myself and my surroundings. I had to live some life, some not-so-good life, so that I could move myself away from the unwanted. I gently led myself forward to better days. It was quite a subtle move. Subtle yet powerful.

No one understands, not even me.

"Is it so bad, then, to be misunderstood? Pythagoras was misunderstood, and Socrates, and Jesus, and Luther, and Copernicus, and Galileo, and Newton, and every pure and wise spirit that ever took flesh. To be great is to be misunderstood."
–Ralph Waldo Emerson, Self-Reliance

Why the hell am I doing this to myself again? This kept running through my mind as I smiled and rolled with the happenings around me. Shaking hands, making small talk with relatives I barely knew and who probably didn't even know whose kid I was. Me sitting there at my daughter's 15th birthday party or better yet quinceanera which was also a combo party of my parents 50th wedding anniversary, so uncomfortable within my own skin, simply by the clothes on my body. Had I understood that my body was screaming, sending S.O.S. signals to listen to myself and what *I* wanted, this story would be written differently or not written at all, but I misunderstood the messages. For months before the party, I had spent some considerable time eating higher calorie foods and switching to a weight training workout, in hopes to gain some weight and not look so skinny. Between the scale and the mirror, I'd gauge my progress, and I'd gained about 15 pounds in eight months, not too shabby for me who stood 5'2" and started at 110 pounds.

The morning of the party I was awakened by a wave of nausea that seemed to land on me out of nowhere. It was so bad that I vomited in my mouth as I jumped out of bed and stumbled into the bathroom. What the fuck was going on? I told myself I wasn't nervous, at least I didn't feel it in my body. So where was this coming from? If I knew then what I know now, I wouldn't have written this book the way I did. My spirit and body were communicating to me from the depths of my soul, what I was truly holding in my heart. And I had misunderstood its guidance. This dress I was wearing was what everyone wanted me to wear and yet, somehow, I was on the losing end by how utterly disgusting I felt. Again? I let myself down again? Well, at least you pleased the family I'd tell myself and yet that lost its saving grace over time. The pony dance wasn't working, it never had, I just fooled myself *every single fucking time.* Misunderstanding led to this, enough was enough, or was it?

Mija, I don't understand why you just don't like dresses. The million-dollar comment from my mother. And I in turn wanted to say, *well I don't either, so now what do we do with this?* Those who misunderstand and the one who is misunderstood, neither is ever wrong, perhaps only in the eyes of the opposite side.

Misunderstood according to Merriam-Webster means "not sympathetically appreciated". Being misunderstood is such a common feeling among us; that much, we do

5

understand. Understanding ourselves and others is hard at times. I'd gathered that I was misunderstood, along with my actions and the course I was taking. Shit, I barely understood myself; how could I have any hope that others would?

I didn't know when or where, but I knew that at the right moment I'd get curious about myself. Curious enough to honor me. And in like, honoring life—the life moving through *me*. Going through this kind of deep shit takes some guts. Therapy is the same; it takes some realization to get you there. We're all doing the same, living as best we know how. We look around and at times mimic what others are doing. Society tends to set the standard, the pace of life. So much is happening around us. And even more is taking place inside of us, in our own little world. We have *our* way of seeing things. There are repetitive voices, thoughts, ideas. A whole production.

If our way of living doesn't fall into a category that has been accepted by society as a whole, we feel left out. We feel misunderstood. Our own take on life should be respected and allowed to take flight. When this way of thinking becomes the new standard, the misunderstood will be applauded for following their unique calling. Take Lady Gaga, for example, she and her wardrobe were misunderstood by many. At the 2010 MTV Video Music Awards she wore a dress made entirely out of raw beef. While the public was split on opinions, she was named by Time as the top fashion statement of 2010. Would you look at that! She weathered through the storms of criticism, harsh words and judgments.

As far as being misunderstood check out what Lady Gaga told her audience at the opening show in Las Vegas on December 28, 2018. First, she gazed into the crowd, no words, just the cheers of her adoring fans. The energy in the place was electrifying. She told them that she loved them dearly and that for a really long time she felt misunderstood as others saw the way she dressed, talked and presented herself as being shallow. And she thanked *them* for birthing *her* as Lady Gaga. Who would've thought.

The crowd won't see that part of the journey, the battles within oneself– of course they won't. Just like one doesn't often see the potential diamond in the coal or the beauty of the fire that refines the gold. There are many things in this life we'll never understand. But our lack of understanding doesn't take away from the greatness of that which is misunderstood, such as Lady Gaga and— especially you.

Write it out.

In my college years I journaled a lot, not fully knowing that I was getting acquainted with myself. It felt innocent and fun, a sure way to empty myself of unhealthy inner content. I held within me, so many questions and concerns about what I was living, as I'm sure you may have too. I felt myself to be a good person, with a good caring heart and I believed that I should be happy. Being good should be noticed and rewarded, right? But what I was experiencing didn't seem to match my goodness. I felt that life didn't make sense. I just wanted to throw my hands in the air as a sign of surrender. What good was being good if there was no payoff for me? It turns out the good I was doing wasn't genuine. It was for someone else's feeling good, and I was doing it to make up for everything I was not. I was being pulled into a vicious cycle.

I sat on the couch of my apartment living room looking at my wedding pictures. With a cup of coffee in one hand and a picture in the other, I glanced at pictures in the album. I looked intently at each and I didn't feel any sense of happiness. I sat back and felt the tears rolling down my face. They flowed steadily for a few minutes and then I began to sob heavily. Those new tears were accompanied by a deep feeling of sadness. I asked myself, "Why the sadness?" I just allowed myself to cry until I couldn't cry anymore. Now came a moment of answering that question– time to put my big girl pants on and be honest. After all, only I could really answer that.

Why the sadness? What was it about those pictures that caused me to react in that way? I knew exactly why, but I had shied away from telling myself the truth in hopes that things would turn out better for me. In a nutshell, my now ex-husband and I never really wanted to get married. We had our daughter out of wedlock and the pressure of our Catholic upbringing led to marriage. I took an action that was not chosen whole-heartedly by me. I took an action that was meant to please the families, so that *I would not go to hell*. All of my choices then, all people pleasing choices.

I've questioned why I was here and why I went through such hurtful experiences. There has been too much really fucked up shit in my head. Expecting the worst wasn't unusual for me. My road to self-discovery wasn't this joyous, skipping down the street kind of beginning. It felt like one day I was just different–not hugely different, but different enough that I noticed. And the difference felt worth following. Writing was teaching me about me, in a very subtle way.

I still wondered how I became who I was. I sort of felt like a stranger to myself. While spending time with myself, my thoughts and feelings, I would have valley lows more than not. The valley lows seemed to be where I spent a lot of my days. In those moments, though, there were still many gifts and doors to open and other paths to walk on.

There were many aspects of my personality that I did not like. It didn't feel good to critique myself of course, but that's just what I did back then. At the same time, I knew deep down that I didn't really believe half the shit I said to and about myself. That was my gut feeling talking to me. I wrote about it a lot. I suppose I felt very strongly about it. It was like other voices were dissing me and yeah I heard my own voice from time to time. I was like *"Really? Is that my own voice joining in on dissing me? Wow. It's gonna be like that huh?!".* But the questions I should have been asking were, "How'd all this get in my head? Who put it there? Did I? Or did I leave a window open at some point and let it sneak in?".

There's something different about writing down your ideas, feelings and emotions. It involves more of our attention. So, I continued to write, to express what I was feeling as honestly as I could. With honesty come many feelings. When I would go back later and read over my entries, it was amazing. I felt like I didn't know the side of me I found on the pages; the writing was so different from the girl I knew as myself. The things I spoke of and expressed in writing really gave me a birds eye view of where my mind was. I could literally see myself slowly changing, growing. The person that had journaled a year before sounded very different from the one that was reading it then. An updated me was interested and intrigued by what the former me had to say; the perspectives were different and that caught my attention.

If you've ever seen the show Hoarders, you understand the many emotional states and challenges that can lead to the accumulation of material things that literally drown people or keep them trapped, physically and emotionally. The therapists always know there is a deeper meaning to what they see. It's not as simple as just saying to the person, "Listen, you just need to snap out of it and see the mess you're living in. How hard can it be?". If that statement alone would do it, great. But it often isn't enough. The individual is living in a cyclical trance and they just don't see it. A zone of comfort has been established and it isn't even comfortable anymore. So the therapists choose to dig. They know the value of it and the release it'll afford. Whatever has been harbored inside the individual needs to be understood and let go of, even if it gets ugly at first. Reminds me of the saying that it's got to get worse before it gets better.

Sometimes revisiting your past and the former versions of yourself isn't the first choice. Perhaps that's why we're led there in a mysterious way, because life knows we want to turn away, missing the lessons, fearing venturing forward. Some spiritual teachers advise not to look at the "dead" past and to focus on the future. The belief is that when you look at past hurt, you invite it in again or give it center stage once more. My mind can understand that concept. But my mind also tells me that there is another side to the coin; taking a peek at the past has its benefits.

My journaling was providing me with more than I realized; it was a real outlet. I was able to hear myself clearer when I wrote. Writing was revealing hidden aspects of me that I could now understand. Digging around in my own dirt seemed necessary, it felt right, and I'm so thankful I did it. Man the things I came to know!

Look closely.

I have so many flashbacks of myself moving through life, my childhood and teenage years. Things didn't make much sense back then. At those ages they often don't. Old pictures were very telling of what I was thinking and feeling then. I could read actually myself, you know? And I didn't like what I was reading. Those former feelings were quite active, so much that they jumped out at me. A part of me could still feel their strength. Those pictures caught a very small glimpse of a moment, just a flash. But the residue of emotions they captured had life in them.

Pictures of younger me tell stories. My eyes, my facial expressions, a story. When I see those pictures I'm taken to the exact emotions my face was expressing in each one. Whatever was going on inside of me, energetically, was coming to the surface. It had to. No smile on my face. Not one real-looking smile, for so many years. That blank stare. Why? That was a great question to pose to myself. It had a hint of freedom in it. And it felt like it led somewhere. Where I had been before left a trail, something I could follow, but I didn't know to pay attention to it. I often avoided taking pictures, as I didn't like to see myself in them. Seeing a sad face isn't very appealing, especially when it's your own. A cemented point in time, ugh, not very cute.

I found a picture of my cousin and I when we were about 12 years old. It was a booth picture and I have no idea where it was taken, but I hated looking at it. In the picture my cousin had her head tilted toward my shoulder and had a huge smile. She seemed happy in the picture. I on the other hand, had this weird numb look on my face. I couldn't help but judge myself for the enormous eyeglasses I was wearing, they practically covered my small face. I seriously thought I was ugly as hell and felt bad for that kid. So bad that I didn't want to look at the picture again; I placed it in a book and onto my bookshelf. Out of sight, out of mind, I told myself.

Now I understand why it's said that even when you're in a room full of people, or with a loved one, you can still feel lonely as fuck! I knew I had felt that, and my face corroborated it. It left hints of where to look for answers. The answers raise their hand and wave for you to turn to them, but sometimes you're so zoned out that you miss the obvious. Finding the courage to zone in was one of the best things I could ever have done for myself. I was on a rescue mission–for me.

Your face and your body language speak without saying a word; they are so communicative. I began to realize that I never really said nice things to myself, even on the deep end of thought. As silly as it may sound, I didn't know how. The days I had spent reading myself in pictures led me to the thoughts that had taken up space for far too long. As soon as I took the time to really read myself, I could hear the nonsense in my head. It was like the clouds in me parted and the light shone in, exactly what I needed to tend to. My mind was literally offering up itself and all the contents it held. It was becoming my friend. It wanted to make peace with me. From a far distance, from this newfound inner kindness, I began to hear gentle whispers. They knew how to make their way through all the clamoring of negative thoughts and comments. They knew that their turn had come up and that I was interested in what I was hearing.

CHAPTER 2

Let My Memory Serve *me*

Checking Out the Dots!

"You can't connect the dots looking forward; you can
only connect them looking backwards. So, you have to
trust that the dots will somehow connect in your future.
You have to trust in something – your gut, destiny,
life, karma, whatever. This approach has never let me
down, and it has made all the difference in my life."
–Steve Jobs

With so many dots of life experiences, where would I
start? I started as far back as my mind could remember.
I went to a place in time when I felt pulled. I couldn't
always tell whether I was being pulled by who I was to
become or by who I was expected to be. The two were
so far from one another.

When I started school around the age of five, I believe
I already realized I had certain qualities that didn't match
up with my parents' expectations. It's crazy to think that
even at such a young age, some of us sense that right away.

We sense there are differences that disconnect us from others. And instead of being valued, these differences often create a bigger separation between ourselves and the people around us.

Me; different from my sisters, different from my mother, different from other females, that's what felt most true. Obviously, I was, since I'm a unique individual. But the difference I speak of here is the kind that divides, the kind that led me to question myself and my own personality. How did the young me know this? I simply watched my mother and sisters. They enjoyed clothing that I did not, fixing their hair in certain ways, using makeup and accessories. When it came to me none of these things interested me. I much rather have my hair in a ponytail and been wearing sweatpants and a t-shirt, ready to get my hands dirty outside.

On Sunday mornings I would watch my mom get ready for church. She'd pick out one of her nicest and most elegant dresses and beautiful shoes to go with it. Sometimes she would take a matching purse and wear expensive looking jewelry. I thought she looked pretty and classy, like a rich lady.

I would often smell perfume coming from my parents' bedroom and I'd walk over to smell some more. My parents' bedroom was really small, just fitting a twin bed and three drawer dresser with a large square-shaped mirror sitting on top. Being the bedroom was so small, I always asked permission before going in. My mom rarely told me no. I would sit on their bed feet dangling. I would closely watch my mom's every move. My mom would apply dots of red lipstick on her cheekbones and with her index and middle finger, gently spread the lipstick to create a blush. Then she'd apply lipstick on her lips, rub

15

them together and boom, she was all set. I loved how she looked. When it came to me doing these things, it was not so enjoyable. I kind of wished I liked all that stuff, dresses, make-up, etc. BUT I JUST DIDN'T. IT FELT AWKWARD ON ME AND FOR ME.

Voices: *No, no, no, go here..no, no, go there. No, no, no… you can't be both!*

Me: *Aaaah! I just wanna' be me.*

I could feel the pull inside of me to join my dad and brothers when they chopped wood outside or did any physical yard work, but I was continually told that women had different expectations such as tending to the household chores and "looking like a lady". Being different was not a highlight; at least that's what I thought. It felt like I was being shoved or forced into things I didn't enjoy. I felt cut off from my mom and sisters in a way that I didn't like and that I wouldn't have chosen– and that feeling was always with me; something I couldn't shake off. Of course I couldn't shake it off. But the me who was created to be just that– *me*–she wasn't going anywhere. Her voice would be heard soon enough.

Tracing some steps

When my thoughts got too loud, or too painful, I held on to them even tighter. I didn't express them to anyone. They weren't cute or joyful. They weren't what I wanted others to see. I was doing my best to keep them contained and by doing so, possibly get rid of them in the process. I was working against myself because how could I be free if I wasn't learning how to let go and release. Bottling up my feelings and concerns just made more sense at the time. I barely understood why I felt so off from everybody else. I had six siblings and two parents at home, so you'd think I would've had a whole array of individuals I could talk to– or at least one out of the eight. But it wasn't quite that way for me. Being the youngest made me feel somehow disconnected. My siblings were all so funny and loving toward me as a kid. Their loving ways have remained the same over the years, and their humor. So why didn't I turn to them? Well, there were things my family said that gave me an inkling that what I wanted to speak up about was not a welcome topic. I would've wanted to talk about my attraction to girls. My dislike of dresses, bows, sequins, ruffles, pretty much anything society deemed "girly".

But my family, unknowingly, would make comments about gay people while watching TV or listening to the radio, that would confuse my young mind. They would say that gay people were demon-possessed, evil, and disgusting. They would especially make bad comments about gay women. *Marimacha* and *joto*, were the words I heard most often. Both are slang terms used amongst Spanish speakers and a derogatory way to address gays. And little 'ol me was one of them, I thought. The environment around me felt unsafe. What was I to do with what I felt inside? Why would I tell them how I felt? How could I? There had to be something wrong with me, I thought. Right away I looked at myself as the bad guy. This feeling of liking girls and not liking to participate as the girl the world wanted created a true internal tug-of-war. I felt a part of me being shoved away, being placed into dormancy. The me who was speaking up through the genuine feelings I had, attraction to girls... I knew it was what came with me as a package, as a human being. But this package deal felt burdensome.

So, there I was, aware of what I felt inside, aware of what society thought about it and very aware of my family's take on it. If both society and my family said that how I felt was "wrong", then they must be "right". Right? I mean, I was only a kid, and they should know more than me; so, I figured I had a big problem on my hands. My only solution at the time was to go with what they said. The real me would have to wait, or maybe never show up. At the time having my family's acceptance meant more than having the freedom to be myself.

When I was about five, my mother told me that she tried to abort me many times. I'm not sure how much influence my aunts had (eleven sisters, yes eleven) but that was the story I was told. My mom would go on to say that my aunts were only looking out for her health, and also, the fact that she already had six children. Not to mention that my mom was 41 and my dad 46 years of age when I was born. Honestly, I never felt bad. My mother also shared that at birth, I had a twin who didn't fully develop. She would jokingly tell me my twin didn't survive because I ate all the food that went into the womb, and the idea that I had harmed my twin made me sad. Little did my mom know that her words made young me carry guilt and shame. I truly don't think that she meant to, but still, some damage was done.

During those years of my childhood, teenage years and even young adult years, I sought their acceptance. I abandoned myself for a lot of years, seeking to please my mom, especially. I wanted her to see beyond my "liking girls" and see me for me. I wanted her to know that I didn't choose to be tomboyish to upset her, and that in no way was I wanting to hurt my family's image. She had to understand that I was not convinced by any other to behave a certain way; it was just my natural identity that was unfolding. I was new to it, too.

Glimpses of me.

I know that I wasn't mimicking anyone or choosing to be an outcast in the family. In a way I felt that my family had the idea that I just wanted to be rebellious. To them being gay was the most controversial way to go.

Five years of life and I was already feeling heavy emotions and even questioning my own existence. So much was going on at that point. I understood very little, but what I felt was true to me. At this point, I believe that whatever differences between us that are singled out as wrong are most likely the truest pieces of who we are. Individuality that is respected and valued, that sounds right and feels good. Individuality that is ridiculed and shamed, that sounds and feels unpleasant. We may not know it in childhood, but we feel it. The different dots connecting and beginning to make sense. Looking briefly at my former years without fear, has allowed the real to feel ever so near.

The differences in me carved some damage on my path of life. They were differences that I felt and saw every day. They divided me, and pulled at me, and I swayed with the tension for too long. As weird as it may sound, I never have been upset at my mom for my internal storms. I know the frustration I grew up feeling was just from not being understood. It's funny how, when things begin to connect–sometimes years later– the picture becomes clearer and understanding rolls out like a red carpet. Damn right I deserve it, roll it out!

Gathering The Pieces of You

The ugly cry. With my eyes closed tightly, hot tears gathered at my chin. I felt the drip of them onto my chest, the stain of the tears growing in circumference on my t-shirt. Fake, fake, fake is what I thought of myself. Such a fake dude! But who was I really faking? Faking about what? About whom I was.

As I was rubbing my sore feet, I glanced at the shoes I had worn the night before and they emphatically screamed 'fake' towards me. Why would they say that? Up to this day of my life I had learned a thing or two about being more of myself, I felt I was more me than ever. By this point, I had openly accepted my sexual orientation, which seemed like an insurmountable obstacle before. So how could I still be a fake? Fake about what this time? Honesty told me I was faking what I said I'd learned. I thought I had learned to accept all of me, which meant I would dress, behave, talk and be just as I wanted. So, what happened? How I fuck this up? Deep down I felt how harsh I was being with myself. I still had room to learn how to be gentle with my own growing pains.

The night before was my daughter's wedding. As beautiful of an evening it was, watching my daughter and son-in-law in love and joyous, my heart cried its own cry. My heart wanted its own joy to dance about, not just the joy of others. What did the shoes have to do with this? The shoes in and of themselves were harmless. They signified an aspect of myself that was still hiding. Those shoes would never be what I would want to buy, let alone wear on my own feet. So then, why did I end up with them on my feet, at my daughter's wedding? I wasn't sure of the answer then because the happiness I felt that day, for my daughter, was genuine indeed. This suggested that I deal with myself at another time. *No, no, no...The time is now. There is never any better time than now. Research yourself, review the footage again,* my mind exclaimed. Red challenge flag got tossed, time for a 'what really happened moment'!

It makes sense that therapy goes deep; therapists are always trying to connect the dots so that they can provide the best treatment for each patient. The look-back factor as I like to call it has benefits. It has to be approached from a place of wanting to do it for the betterment of yourself, not as a punishment. *You* must want it and seek it out. Like they say, "You can lead a horse to water but you can't make him drink."

The time and place for the hurt has already come and gone. Why would we seek to burn ourselves again, we might ask? I don't believe any of us does—but we do it anyway. Looking back and changing nothing keeps the hurt alive. Talking them over with friends and wallowing does the same thing. It feels nice that your friends hear you out, but sometimes all they hear is a broken record.

This way of living is easy to fall into. It keeps us focused on how life has beat us up, and it allows us to give up any real responsibility for improving. We point to the injuries our past has left behind and explain how those same injuries pave the road we walk on. As long as we are alive, though, we are moving forward, and the past has so many dots that can connect in a positive way. I told myself to let life explain itself and to trust the process. And here I am, doing just that. A little silence pays dividends.

STEP INSIDE WHERE IT'S QUIET

CHAPTER 1

Silence IS golden

"Silence is the root of everything. If you spiral
into its void, a hundred voices will thunder,
messages you long to hear."
–Rumi

As life moved on, I noticed the energy I once used
to house wasn't very enjoyable or pleasant. The uneasy
feeling seemed to always be there, and I felt consumed by
it. I didn't seem to belong anywhere since I was juggling
acting like a heterosexual and keeping my gayness on
the sidelines. The angst was real. My own company was
uncomfortable; I wasn't settled. I felt miserable a whole
lot. I would never admit then that the misery I was feeling
had a lot to do with me playing it safe. But safe for who?
Because I sure didn't feel safe. Why didn't I do anything
about it? Was I just not aware that I could?

In the luxury of having days to myself, I liked to be
in silence sometimes. It wasn't a planned thing, but more
like a gut instinct that led me to do it. It was kind of weird
at first, because I wasn't really used to being in silence.

I felt a bit uncomfortable with being alone. Growing up, our home was always loud, with music playing and people chatting, maybe even the TV on for no reason. Silence wasn't easy to get, and alone time was almost impossible. I personally preferred a loud environment over silence. I could hide in all the noise. I don't know if you've noticed but the voice in your head seems louder when you're in silence, like it suddenly gets hold of a microphone and realizes it loves it. It also wants answers from you. I guess the day-to-day was a bit too loud; I never heard my mind so clearly until I gave silence a try.

The silence for me felt different of course, it was awkward, and I didn't know what to do with myself during that quiet time. Being with myself felt like being left alone with a stranger not a whole lot of conversation going on at first. The chatter that was taking place, I no longer wanted to hear, there were just too many negative comments floating around in there. It was like hanging out with a bully. When quiet came, I would think, "I'm just gonna' get beat up." I never saw it as worthwhile. But I was just so young, I had a lot to learn. That insatiable desire to feel good would show me and teach me in the silence. Having been afraid to visit with my own thoughts seems silly in hindsight.

> "I closed my mouth and spoke to you
> in a hundred silent ways."
> –Rumi

Silence would take on a new twist, too, allowing me to feel like God was ever more present. A sense of connection with the Creator enveloped me in peace. No inspirational songs, no speeches, no sounds– just me being still and feeling a little bit better than I did before. It was so simple, just closing my eyes and venturing into the silence within myself. Eventually it felt safe.

Now I know what to do, better and better each day. This is a game I definitely want to play! You should too. It's a game that always begins, exists and ends in the stillness of yourself. You can always hear best in the silence.

Deep thought comes over me, so
I draw within. A silence.
A place of reflection, of careful
and loving introspection.
Allow all that you know to cover you and your affairs.
Allow yourself to move from the
perspective of who you truly are.
There's no rush at all in the present moment.
Inside is the magic that soothes.

Go ahead and dictate the projection screen of your mind. Express yourself radiantly. You know that you know; you feel it. You feel it most of the time, because it has led you here. Be very happy with yourself. In fact: congratulations for being wonderfully you.

~

Peace and Quiet.

The mental chatter is not easy to ignore; there is a lot of it going on sometimes. It's just like being in a busy airport. You can hear a multitude of voices, noises and otherwise; yet you're also tuning in to hear about your flight.

In the past I was not really tuning in to my true voice; I was hearing all the other noise, but not listening to my best self. I was giving my attention to worst-case scenarios and hearing the worst things. My mind appeared to conform to the beliefs I'd grown up with. My mind didn't want to part with them. It somewhat felt easier to just do the same old same old.

The world I was living in had a pattern and not all of it seemed beneficial for me to continue following. My mind sought to be renewed, so that my life could be transformed. New conversations were sparked within me. Questions came up that were new to me. For example, how could I adjust my thoughts? How could I stop thinking about what I didn't want to think about?

The questions began cropping up at a random early morning. Getting up early was kind of a big deal for me since I'm naturally a night owl– so waking up with new interesting questions was attention-grabbing. And actually, enjoying waking up early was another big deal!

Be on the lookout for those moments when you feel the need to change something in your day, or when a question pops up that is totally new. My quiet moments feel so valuable because they truly are valuable. Enjoying my time alone feels to me as if the higher me is tapping me on my shoulder, ready to speak some more wisdom. You don't hear shit from yourself audibly, you know, but you sure do hear all the talking in the brain! And damn, it's a lot sometimes. I'll tell myself to pipe down up there, or I'll even shush myself. I'm way more aware of what's going on in my head than ever before. I mean, this time around, I truly give a fuck about which ideas are taking up space inside me and what I am doing with my life, with me every day. I'm learning to ride the ups and downs, and to fully utilize the wisdom in each.

In these little chill moments, I carve out for myself, life feels calm. All the noise of any concerns I have seems to be silenced. I don't feel like tripping out and getting all worked up with worry. I tell myself to just relax through all of it– I mean, what can it hurt? My former tendency to get all bent out of shape and lose my day to feeling down was just dumb. When I can remind myself of this, I feel better. I feel like I care. I do care. And because I care, I see so much in my life to admire. I like to slow down and ponder what a good life I have. Every single aspect of our everyday life has an innumerable amount of things to feel thankful for. So, start counting.

In the morning now, I chill in bed for a while and feel how good it feels to feel good. To feel the comfort of my pillow, the sheets providing the right temperature, the bed oh so cozy– oh man, thank you! I love to start amping up my feeling good as soon as I awaken. I know I didn't ever do that before. Before, I would wake up instantly picking up from where I left off the previous day. I'd wake up and right away feel worry, anger or sadness– definitely not the business. And yet again, I did this for a long time.

If you don't show yourself that you are of utmost importance, then why would someone else do it for you? I know that sometimes we feel certain people bring something to us that almost feels like they saved us or rescued us. And that's true enough, once in a while. But we all need to get to that place of self-sufficiency. It's the best way to play in life. I now play differently, because I know that I must care. I have to set the standard of what feeling good looks like, what it sounds like. I owe it to myself to prove myself. Things now stay very interesting, and the fun just keeps coming in from every direction.

I love to remind myself to just close my eyes as much as I need, to go home for a bit, within myself, where I am always in full control.

~

Private Talks

"But when you pray, go away by yourself, shut the door behind you, and pray to your Father in private. Then your Father, who sees everything, will reward you."
—Matthew 6:6 NLT

PRAYER is an art and requires practice. The first requirement is a controlled imagination. Parade and vain repetitions are foreign to prayer. Its exercise requires tranquility and peace of mind. "Use not vain repetitions," for prayer is done in secret and "thy Father which seeth in secret shall reward thee openly."
—Neville Goddard, Prayer: The Art of Believing

It has been said that prayer is us telephoning God, the Creator. The conversation becomes a very personal interaction with the very breath that breathes life into your body, that created your physical form and sustains you. That prayer is the ongoing conversation of life. Shut the door of your physical senses from time to time and participate in this conversation. You'll reap the reward of feeling amazing when picturing something good for yourself. When you can hear it, smell it, feel it, taste it, touch it, and see in your mind's eye, you win all around. You've held the feeling of what you desire with all its joy. You get to feel good now and put something in the bank for later. The day you meet with the picture in your mind, you are rewarded yet again. You gift unto yourself and others. And all of it is done in a secret place where you and the creator chill together in silence.

I've heard before that the eyes are the windows of the soul. They convey so much information. They speak without saying a word, they give you a glimpse of what's inside. Closing that door of the eyes lets you right into the chamber of your innermost self, exactly where you need to be— that secret place where you're planted and where you get to tend to, if you haven't already. It's all good if you see a patch of weeds or a desolate place; the most favorable thing here is that you are in your garden and can do as you please there.

It seems to me that this secret place is where the show of life is being run. But it's so secretive that even we may not know it exists for some time. Or we think we don't know, but some deep gut feeling tells us the secret is inside of us, unique and personal. The secret place leaves hints and impressions on us, those that rise to the surface and offer much valuable insight. A little careful exploration can go a long way.

Let's see what else is in here!

I knew the visit I had taken into my own mind and memory was something I wanted to do often. A part of me knew that one visit would not suffice. Each day carries within it so many activities that can distract and derail us.

Like exercise is needed to maintain good physical health, my mind required its own check-ups to keep healthy. No one visits the doctor only once and claims a clean bill of health. The doctor's expertise is needed to see exactly what's going on inside the physical body as you age. And you and I are experts when it comes to ourselves and what we think.

A friend, a family member or even a therapist can visit some aspects of you and help shed some light. That is always welcome of course but ownership of self is a wonderful thing; you have the right to make all the necessary moves to best suit you. And only you can honestly see what else you hold inside. Don't hesitate to check in often and tune yourself up. Dancing to a different tune you'll soon see reveals the truth of what your life seeks to be.

Rules, regulations, how-to's, beliefs, laws, steps to take...so much information floating around. Everyone offers their insights and views on how to live life, how to achieve certain goals, a step-by-step process to success and happiness. Everyone has something to say about everything.

There is an enormous amount of information constantly flowing around and about us. We take in and hold on to so much. Anything that has been held tightly and that now hurts needs to be revisited for sure. We outgrow certain ideas and beliefs as we move through life. Sometimes you have to check your own intentions. It's good to wonder where you're coming from when you act in a certain way. I've seen that the more I stand firm on believing something new, the better I feel. Giving myself a chance to really live up to what I believe makes it easier to review my own belief system.

If I don't start evicting from my mind the expired concepts, I leave no room for my growth. When an idea causes us emotional pain, it's worth investigating. Be interested in yourself. Give yourself a fair chance to change something for the better.

In the stillness of a quiet moment, you may find that you hear yourself with such clarity. Some of your thoughts will make you cringe, but the bright side is that you get to toss out the stuff that hurts you. It's kind of like having to apply the sniff test to refrigerated food. You may cringe at some of what you find. It's best to toss out the old shit!

You might not even realize you need to, until life suddenly doesn't seem enjoyable. Some experience this at a very young age. Who even thinks they are carrying extraneous or rotting stuff at such a young age? I know I didn't. This can be a bit more challenging, since we can't sniff out unhealthy or toxic beliefs or ideas, but we sure can *feel* them. And even though I was young of age, my feelings of confusion felt off, they felt unnatural.

When I worked alongside my parents in the fields as a kid, picking table grapes mostly, I heard many comments that I wasn't sure were good or bad. At the moment I didn't feel any strong emotion either way.

I don't recall being spoken to very often; the information was just being thrown out there and landing on me. It could have been that, because I was the youngest of the seven kids, everyone felt I wouldn't understand. I'm sure there were things I didn't need to know— and neither the adults nor I could imagine the long-term effects their words would have. Some of what they said certainly wasn't nice.

There I was, a little kid, picking up on everything. I was like a sponge and simply doing what a sponge is meant to do: absorb. In the childhood years, it's natural for us to spend most of our time picking up on our surroundings, absorbing others' comments, beliefs, ideologies before we're even old enough to test anything out for ourselves. I was just gathering everything along the way in life– the good, the bad and the ugly.

The good thing is that, eventually, the time comes to ring out the life sponge and prepare to absorb new and better ideas. Every sponge must be emptied so that it can pick up more. Wringing out your own mind and what's been dropped in there is actually rather fun. You get to experience the feeling of relief. And then a little build-up of excitement comes around and cheers you on for making room for better.

Realizing that all that gathered stuff of life was not necessarily chosen or gathered by you invites a feeling of freedom. What's been thrown at you can finally be sorted through. I pondered on this for some time. I hoped that maybe, just maybe, I could shake off the sadness I felt. Something was telling me that the hurt I had grown up with was worth looking at in a new light.

In the middle of whatever fucked-up moment I was living, it wasn't always easy to absorb anything new. I was full of foreign beliefs that seemed to bring pain, and I was fixated. There was some sifting to do, to move the "extra", crappy shit out of my mind. The extraneous is "the irrelevant" according to Merriam-Webster. Irrelevant ideas to who I truly was. Yep, that's exactly right!

Time to Get the Juicer Out!

So, there was young me with all she'd picked up; she claimed it every day. She believed she had to lug it around because it belonged to her and made her who she was. But she was full of emotions that didn't feel good. The uneasiness was there, inside, with me all the time. In one of his lectures, self-help author and motivational speaker Dr. Wayne Dyer asked "What comes out of you when you are squeezed?" He went on to explain that when you squeeze an orange, orange juice will come out. You know exactly what the orange contains inside, so when you squeeze it, there is no surprise. We think that we know what others are about. We even think we know all of ourselves– until the squeeze factor comes into play.

Life has squeezed me, and with every squeeze, caused by painful experiences, it has showed me exactly what I was carrying within. Certain behaviors, words, mindsets, ideas, beliefs all have been extracted– and not all were pleasant, I can tell you. It seems almost shocking when we carry on in ways that even we don't like.

Understanding the bullshit, so we don't end up surprised by what comes out of us when we are squeezed, is so important. I see that getting it out on my own, instead of letting it build up, is way better. If and when it does come out of us in a blowout fashion, though, we simply must navigate the learning curve and pick ourselves up.

Nowadays, I purposely choose to say, "Go ahead and squeeze me!". I want to better understand what the fuck I've held inside for too long– those things that have no more value left in them yet keep showing up. When I ask this of life, of myself, just for a few seconds, I reflect.

That's usually followed by a huge sigh of relief, because now I can see everything for what it is. The truth of me being exposed is what I now expect.

My past behavior of holding in so much made me afraid to express myself. It was a pretty dark time, hiding within myself. A part of me grew angry at the sham of what I'd become. "The straw that broke the camel's back," was the best way to describe my eruptions– all the little things I never dealt with, just adding up, then overtaking me. The anger felt like it was making me go insane. I just acted like a fool for a lot longer than necessary. And even worse, sometimes I didn't even learn anything from it. The explosion felt somewhat good at the moment. However, the relief was very short-lived, and ultimately, exploding was embarrassing and resolved nothing.

Everyone will handle what comes out in their own way, since everyone has been poured into differently. Everyone has gathered what they have gathered, wanted and unwanted, good and bad. What we do and what we say...it has a starting point; it has a foundation from where it springs up. Cleaning that up is really a gift to yourself: another step toward getting to the real you.

~

CHAPTER 2

Behind the scenes

Metaphysical teachers will say that feelings are our compasses, always showing the emotional location we are at and the direction those emotions are taking us. Given that statement and having tested it out in researching myself, I conclude that they indeed are serving us. Our emotions are ours to understand and to choose. We all have them and act differently on them. They want to express themselves.

When I close my eyes, it's a perfect time to sense what I am feeling. No matter what it might be, it's really nice to check in with myself. Sometimes, I feel calm; other times I feel a bit frantic. I can tell if I'm out of balance, tipped too far to either side of an emotion. I used to always feel a need to rush and fix it. I didn't realize I was feeling so many things at once that clashed.

I've learned to just chill for a bit and then see what conversations are going on inside of myself. I like to take a look at what images I'm seeing, as well. It's really fascinating what your mind will project throughout the day. And realizing where it's chilling most of the time is quite revealing.

Chillin': It promotes the silence that teaches and reinforces.

So where was my mind kicking it most of the day(s)? I was interested in retracing some steps. Knowing how I felt was the beginning. Owning up to it wasn't always easy, but it did get easier. I've had to face all the impressed ideas that were fueled by low self-esteem, jealousy and lack of confidence. All these emotions did their job. And when they all were given room to play in my mind, they did. A time would come when all the rehearsing in my mind's eye would lead to the curtains being raised so I and others could see what had been happening "behind it all". Think about your own set and scenes. Who is really putting on this play? This play of your life? Oh– it's you. I star in my play. You star in yours. Keep your mind as cool, calm and collected as possible and walk a new walk onto the stage. Change up what's going on behind the scenes of everyday life.

I was calling out to myself from behind it all. I could feel it. And in quiet times, I would begin to hear it. My mind was seeking to be renewed and freed from heavy, unpleasant thoughts. It really wanted to rehearse something new because the old script just wouldn't do anymore. In that background I began hearing myself out (really hearing myself out), spotting repetitive behavior, looking closely at pictures, conjuring up experiences and what they felt like, caring about myself picking up all the pieces to the greater puzzle that is me!

We all play.

> "Most people consider life a battle, but
> it is not a battle, it is a game."
> —Florence Scovel Schinn,
> *The Game of Life and How to Play It*

What game are you speaking of you ask. And what is it that you now know what to do? Life, that game. Living it as a game. Enjoy your participation in it and always be ready to play any role that you are called to play—playing it to the very best of your ability. When interest mixes in with your everyday happenings, life begins to take on the joys of a game. And in this game of life, we play the center role. We play all roles actually, it's our game, our life after all.

So, what is that you are doing now? That which you say you are doing better and better each day.

You know, there's a medley of things I do now, but the one that captivates me every morning and throughout my days is to ask myself how I am feeling. And then the banger is to answer honestly. No point in asking if you're not going to be open about it. This gives me a jump start on where my mood is, on what my vibe is at that very moment. It isn't always happy and jumping for joy and I've figured out that that's ok, perfectly ok. The real deal is getting an honest response from myself so I can best guide myself to something, anything that feels more like what I know myself to be. And I've come to know myself to be perfectly me.

It can go something like this:

Lil' voice: "Good morning me. How are you feeling right now?"

Me: "I'm feeling good. This bed is so freaking cozy. The sheets are the perfect temperature, so cooling and oh so soft, like satin. These pillows make me feel like I'm lying on a cloud, so carefree and peaceful. I feel calm; the image of a serene pond fills my mind. The waters so still, you can see your own reflection, so still that a leaf falls and creates a ripple effect that seems endless. I feel so, so good. Like I got the Midas touch."

Lil' voice: "Wow, that's great!"

Me: "Yes, it is. Feels good to just feel good without anything necessarily happening, other than me expressing how good I feel."

Lil' voice: "Let your feelings of joy now splash all over your day and onto every step you take!

Magnetize by the good feelings you've amassed in thought. Think good, feel good. Feel good, think good. Keep it going, keep it going, keep it going. Enjoy!"

And then there's the flip side of the check-in:

Lil' voice: "Hello, hello me. How are we feeling?"

Me: "Hold on, hold on, I'm still thinking about that one thing that's stressing me out."

Lil' voice: "Ok, but how are you feeling?"

Me: "Not so good. I feel confused about what choice to make. I'm feeling down on myself since I haven't budged on deciding what to do. Ah!!!"

Lil' voice: "So, not feeling your best huh?"

Me: "Nope, not at all. Damn, I gotta figure this shit out! I feel so lost!"

Lil' voice: "Well, I know that you're not feeling good right now but how about telling me about your cat?"

Me: "My cat? What does he have to do with anything?"

Lil' voice: "Perhaps everything. Just answer the question. One thing about your cat, tell me."

Me: "Umm, ok. My cat is a sweetheart. He loves to cuddle next to me no matter where I am, he must make sure he touches me whenever he's close by. He's so loving."

Lil' voice: "Is that a smile I see? Yes, it is, I see a smile."

Me: "Yeah, I'm smiling. Damn you, I'm smiling. But I still got this decision to make, so back to square one!"

Lil' voice: "I know the decision making is still awaiting you, I got that down. Do you think that as you make your way to deciding something that you rather do it from where you are, frustrated and lost, or maybe, just maybe

Paula A. Bravo

take a time out, ponder on how awesome your cat is and then revisit your situation?"

Me: "Obviously I don't enjoy feeling bogged down and unsure, I'm just not sure how my cat is going to help with this."

Lil' voice: "So, really, it's not about your cat. It's about any topic that can lead you to feeling better now. It can be a fluttering butterfly that catches your eye and gives you 30 seconds of peace of mind. It can be a cute fuzzy puppy learning how to walk, wobbling, that makes you giggle. For that moment in time, you felt good. From that position you stand to make a better choice."

Me: "I guess you're making some sense. My cat always makes me feel good, even if I'm just thinking of him. And I do love to see a butterfly move about with such ease and elegance of flight. I mean, what can it hurt to just try this out?"

Lil' voice: "There you go! The smallest of tweaks over time leads to big changes. So proud of you!"

Me: "Thanks. Just talking alone got me feeling way better. Oh, and there's my cat!"

Little by little, as the days come to you, apply all that you understand and be eager to understand even more as you live…it's inevitable, so enjoy the ride!

Silent work

Inner conversations 24/7, even while you sleep. Check in on those talks. What are they saying? How do you feel about what you hear? Do you realize what you are saying, thinking, feeding into all of it, even the sucky stuff?

Why do you live your life the way you do? Why do you think the way you do? Do you believe it can be good, your life? Do you believe in being more than a human with a story? You are breathing right now. Most of the time we don't think about that, it's just a 'what it is' thing. Seriously, it's pretty fucken awesome. Taking the time to stop and consider this might seem silly to some or plain stupid, 'like what's the point?'. Well, it's one way to get your mind off the darker side of life, the side where you feel you usually lose. 'I don't get it' you might think. So here I go to explain myself.

When I stop to chill for a bit, even if just seconds, and pay attention to my breathing by focusing on taking deep, slow breaths, I'm in a neutral zone. You know what I mean? For that moment I'm just chilling. My mind will attempt to do me a favor by reminding me of all the shit I need to worry about. It thinks it's doing me a favor, it can't differentiate because it has done this so often for so long. I think of returning the favor by telling my mind that it's ok to lay low for a bit. Nothing bad is going to happen. It's more like a mini vacay, on me!

'But my life's problems aren't going to fix themselves just by me noticing my breathing!', ok little skeptical part of you. Can you allow yourself a chance to try something new? Something different? This breathing thing is so personal and easy to do. A quick way to part the clouds and let a little sunshine in. Your brain will thank you for it. Everyone enjoys pulling back the curtains and letting some light into a new day, a new idea.

> *"Then the Lord God formed the man*
> *from the dust of the ground.*
> *He breathed the breath of life into*
> *the man's nostrils, and*
> *The man became a living person."*
> *−Genesis 2:7 NLT*

Right now, think about 'your' right now. Notice your breathing. Focus on it more and more. Do your very best to focus on breathing. Let that be the only thing that you are interested in, right now. The world around you, as you know, is doing its thing, moving, keeping busy. Pulling yourself away might be new for some of us. Some of us might not want to pull ourselves into a 'quiet zone'. In the silence, noises seem louder, and those noises might be painful to hear. The crazy thing is that ignoring them isn't making you feel any better. The moment of confrontation is one that some of us rather avoid. But we all know the dangers of ignoring something that can only get better by confrontation. Don't we all rather come face to face with the defeating thoughts that seem to run wildly through our minds?

The moment we chill, notice our breathing, calm the fuck down, is always a good time to do this 'confrontation' thing. You're only confronting yourself, so be bold and gentle. You may not fully know yourself in all of your God given glory, but you can. Chill, breathe slowly, calm the fuck down and undo what needs to be undone and build what is awaiting to be built. Your mind is your soul's playground, have fun!

Just sitting quietly. The room is quiet, with no particular noise to focus on. Your own breath you can hear softly. You're paying attention to it more than you ever really do. You feel your belly move up and down, along with your chest. The beats of your heart, you can sense them as well. For a moment you are feeling just you and you alone. Perhaps some thoughts have been floating around while you've sat quietly. You realize that if there is any noise it's only internally. The dial button is only available to you from here, only you have the right to move it; you have all access. Knowing just how boss you are makes you wanna' pop your collar. Justifiably so.

Rehearse something new

But what about this problem, that person, those bills, tomorrow's troubles and how bad I feel right now? What about that? Sitting quietly never fixed any of it we say. And we say it angrily and with a scared and broken heart. There is a sense of being defensive about it. How dare someone tell me to just sit quietly and see what's up! Sitting doing nothing, yeah ok, whatever!

Ok, so be stubborn about it and go along with what you've always done and then we'll meet up in a year from now and go over our lives. I'm sure it's safe to say that I'll be hearing much of the same from you. I'll look back and hardly recognize my old self, while respecting the growth.

In sitting quietly I'm not saying that by just sitting there all your life's problems will be solved or go away with a wave of a wand. Of course, we all wish that could instantly take place. That's why we all enjoy cartoons or sci-fi movies, it lets our imagination have some play. What I am saying is that a moment of solitude where you can escape for five minutes or so, is just what we all need to remind ourselves how important we are. Merriam-Webster states that important means *of great significance or value.* How often do you tell yourself that you are important? How about telling yourself that you are of great significance so therefore you will now do x, y and z? I mean if we've never told ourselves these things then maybe the five minutes of sitting quietly doesn't sound so full of fluff and stuff.

Oh that's 'odd people shit', 'they're fucken weird', 'she's into tarot and psychic bullcrap', 'he's too spiritual', 'what do crystals even do', 'I don't think they believe in Jesus', 'they believe in crazy stuff', and on, and on, and on. Let's just face it, when presented with ideas that are not ours or familiar to our life we slam them with all types of comments. Why do we feel the need to do that? Who cares really. When we ask why, trust and believe that a whole slurry of reasons will jump out at you.

So, when I say I advise spending five minutes of quiet time, you can have your say on why you think it's smart or stupid. You will wrestle with the idea that you have presented to yourself, while I just rest with the creation of what is mine. My original idea is still as fresh as when it arrived and as eager as a seed when it hits the ground and is ready to thrive!

Five minutes, then another five minutes and another five minutes more. You are significant enough to rack up those five-minute love drops. Drops of love for five minutes. Who doesn't want that? They can be 1 minute love drops every 30 minutes or 10-minute love drops every hour! The whole point is to amp it up. While all the shit is still around you, you will see that you feel better even though shit hasn't changed. Wait, what? Feeling better but what I see looks the same. Hmmm. Keep on feeling better and you will allow yourself to see what looks the same, from a different angle. But if it's the same how's the angle help? Giving yourself a chance to move around in your thoughts pays off big time. You want to be the person that has looked at all the views and has made an informed decision because of it. IN-FORM. (to give facts or information; tell)

Take for example a picture that was captured by the media of Prince William. One angle showed him waving at the greeting crowd, while another angle of the same moment captured Prince William flipping off his fans! The first picture was an accurate account of things, but if one had been adamant about just seeing the one snapshot, we'd be robbed of the truth of the matter. This makes it easier to understand why some people are set on believing what they believe even when presented with information that debunks their truth. They'd be robbed of *their truth* if they allowed themselves to see new evidence.

Sitting quietly has its own truths, its own intrinsic value. All the answers are in there along with the questions, problems and their solutions are there too. When we show up, they all show up as well.

Roll the Tapes!

> "I am who I am. Say this to the people
> of Israel: I am has sent me to you."
> –Exodus 3:14 NLT

"I yam what I yam", is how I first heard this message in the cartoon Popeye. It didn't have too huge of an impact on me, when I first heard it. When I read it in the Bible many years later as a young adult, it was still not impactful. It sounded confusing and like it wasn't really saying anything important. But nonetheless, this scripture had made itself known to me. And in seeking to understand the statement "I am that I am", much unraveling would take place. It was complex and yet simple. Be self-aware, self-confident and self-accepting; that's exactly what Popeye was telling us in his classic statement. It was a statement of ownership. What was I owning up to? Who did I say I was?

I am: the first claim of who we say we are. Geesh, if you put it that way, then scratch some of my first claims; I want to start again. I want to pick better. Because based on what I was hearing in my head, my standards for life were pretty low.

As I kept playing this little game of extracting my old thoughts from tough experiences, I saw what was going on. It literally was whatever I was saying it was. I am this and that. It was so easy to say, "See, I told you I was right. I'm always broke." I guess I wanted people to side with me and ride with me during my down days. What the fuck? Why? Misery loves company? I mean, that makes sense, doesn't it? So, I was right– so what? There are these times when you are indeed right, but what you're right about isn't satisfying.

CHAPTER 3

The tough times and the silence

Oh the woes!

"Consider it pure joy, my brothers and sisters, whenever
you face trials of many kinds, because you know
that the testing of your faith produces perseverance.
Let perseverance finish its work so that you may
be mature and complete, not lacking anything."
—James 1:2-4 NIV

Consider it pure joy to do what? When you face lots
of trials in life? Really? Nope. That just made no sense,
absolutely none. Like, how the fuck? Well, I couldn't
grasp the concept because I had already created a mental
roadblock to that level of understanding. The idea of
hardship being beneficial couldn't make it to my front
door, let alone join my belief stream. Even if it had my
cell number, I'd probably block it there too! I had yet
to understand, but within every difficulty there was
clarification, awaiting my recognition. The difficulties
I would eventually learn, would provide me a chance to

change up my response, to outgrow the old and work out my faith muscles. But the feeling of overwhelm that would often arise, the heaviness in my chest, sometimes was just too much. I automatically knew that this feeling sucked; I didn't want it. And I kept replaying hurtful words and looks of disappointment, feeling uneasy, all the while not truly understanding that replaying all that shit didn't change it. It was still shitty. It was still shitty because all I was doing was focusing intently on the problem alone, not the lesson contained within it.

I always used to say that I didn't want to allow a bad experience to just roll through my life and bitch-slap me and leave it at that. What I meant was that I believed each difficult situation offered me a new insight, a lesson. I wasn't going to allow myself to "lose out on learning" is what I thought, but that wasn't always what I was living. But fuck it. This was for me, for my life, so I had to change up. Literally making peace with all the shit I wished hadn't happened gave me a feeling of overwhelm in my heart too: the good kind.

No one wants to feel bad on purpose. It's much easier to chalk up feeling bad to someone else's actions or words or a painful life experience. When someone tells you to "stop feeling bad", though, it isn't always very welcomed and doesn't always help. Obviously, you want to feel better, but you're not in the right zone for taking in such advice at the moment. You're in the sulking zone, where other people's words bounce right off you. Deep down, we really do want to stop feeling bad, but that auto-pilot reaction is a habit we've picked up along the way. Realizing it's just that– a habit that can be broken– helps us know we can change it.

I went through many moments of betrayal toward

myself. I knew better than to just hurt. But I'd practiced that behavior over and over, and it felt like a natural way to react. There it was, the betrayal, me not even attempting to see any good in a tough situation. Me just riding the one wave of pain. "No thanks, I'll just take all the bad stuff please," said no healthy person ever. Yet we do say it in an unspoken way, via the attention and focus we give.

I pushed away many opportunities for gaining insight and a greater understanding. And since I only pushed them away, they would make their way back to me eventually. This was a great time to reconsider my old game plan of life.

Growing pains.

"Most people are afraid of suffering. But suffering is a kind of mud to help the lotus flower of happiness grow. There can be no lotus flower without the mud."
–Thích Nhất Hạnh, No Mud, No Lotus:
The Art of Transforming Suffering

"Sometimes when you are in a dark place you think you have been buried, but actually you've been planted."
–Christine Caine

Hey, little seed, now into the darkness you go, don't be frightened, you have all you require within yourself (shell). For in the darkness, you'll grow. As small as you appear to the naked eye, I have intelligently woven a beautiful tapestry inside of you. What doesn't seem to make sense holds within it great treasures, so be delighted.

The ground around you may feel fully supportive of you, having the richest nutrients, or it may be a bit dry and tough– but this does not dismay the power you hold, the power that is inside.

Growth is inevitable; remember that when you feel that life is dragging you. Go with the flow of that growth and rejoin the ride. Why the darkness, you ask. The darkness serves its purpose, when you feel this truth, you allow it to do its job. It has its own purpose to serve. Balance demonstrates itself here, for your understanding and remembrance.

Don't keep the darkness hostage. Let it run its natural course– but whatever you do, don't entertain it longer than needed. The darkness that you'll see doesn't desire to stay, just as the ground doesn't desire to keep the seed there.

They have their own flow, lessons to teach; this is their excitement. What appears dark truly is of service. No longer call it the bad guy. It's more like the robin hood of life. Taking from the rich soil and feeding you when you feel poor in faith.

Why you hittin' yourself?

"And the day came when the risk to remain tight in a bud was more painful than the risk it took to blossom."
–Anais Nin

The darker days. The days when you feel anything but happy. The moments that cause emotional and physical pain even– they hit hard. Feeling so unhappy catapulted me into the realm of thinking that maybe I could actually be happy, genuinely happy, just like I'd desired for so long. My feeling of discomfort in my own skin most of the time needed to be addressed. I felt bound by shackles I could not see, shackles of insecurity. Keeping myself brewing on what I conceived as flaws, such as my sexual orientation, only allowed the emotional pain to grow. My wings of self- expression were being tied down and it hurt. I knew I was tired of problem after problem and feeling like shit. I felt I was being tugged, weighed down. The happy moments didn't seem to be sufficient to enjoy for more than a day or two. I had a little bit of happiness sprinkled here and there. It's funny that we settle for so little sometimes– but, then again, that little bit is just enough to sustain us; it works itself out.

Me being me shouldn't have felt so difficult. Me not being me was what made it that way. I had no idea. I had no idea that not being myself was causing so much of my hurt. I felt as if I didn't know how to go about changing or fixing it. Regardless of my confusion, though, life would move me forward, using certain experiences to guide me. And continually reminding me to not hold on so tight, because that might just be what is causing the prolonged pain. Gotta' let go so we can naturally grow.

The rougher experiences made me sure I was out of place, with happiness always at a distance; but in hindsight, they did open the way for me to want to live better. They helped me learn to give more of a fuck. Just as the mud opens the way for the lotus flower to show its beauty, my heartaches and regrets were my nurturing ground. I was planted in a beautiful messy way but that planting had all the right components for me to blossom.

Hold on, let me look at this again.

> "I make friends with hindrances and every
> obstacle becomes a stepping-stone."
> –Florence Scovel Shinn,
> Your Word is Your Wand

Staring at the supplemental property tax bill is all I could do. The county wanted $900 of which I didn't have. I could feel the sweat on my upper lip and starting to build on my forehead. The internal heat of fear and panic was turning up. I decided to get a second cup of coffee. It was the only thing I could think of that didn't make me feel like panicking. I clenched the bill in my left hand as I held my cup of coffee in my right hand. Pain and pleasure. And don't forget to throw in some frantic panic.

What am I gonna' do? Where am I going to get an extra $900? Why didn't I prepare better? What if I lose the house? What if I sell some jewelry at the pawn shop? Or maybe borrow from a check cashing store? Or I could get a personal bank loan? Maybe I could get a second job, fast? If I borrow $200 from so and so, and another $200 from my mom, then I just need to come up with $500. That's still a lot, fuck! Ok, ok…just pay it late. But the late fees dude, they're insane! I can't do that to myself! Poor me, I'm already struggling and now this!

It's hard to believe now how much I allowed problems to send me into overdrive and overthinking. And the sad thing is that all that overthinking was spent on wallowing and panic. There were so many helpful insights I wasn't ready to pick up on then because I was caught up in the pain aspect of it all. That's the only part I understood. That's usually the way it works, too; our focus gets stuck.

At first glance, life struggles can seem one-sided, offering only pain. It's the first wave that crashes down on us. The other side of the struggle offers to refresh you and build you up, if you choose. It reminds us all to be nicer to ourselves at every given moment, because we'll be all the wiser after the storm(s).

In revisiting the more difficult times in my life, I no longer felt sad or scared. I didn't look at them, but through them, because doing that led to a deeper understanding. I wanted to know why the former versions of me were thinking and feeling a specific way. To be honest, my mind was on autopilot for a lot of my youth too, and I never had any inkling that I should– or could– question its thoughts.

But now I know. After every trial, I gained wisdom. It was there for the grabbing. Always. Why stay with the hurt for longer than is beneficial, then? Habit, really. Thinking about it the same way, from the same angle, makes it easy to see that the outcome will be the same. Befriending the hurt over the years has become a tool, one that continues to refine me, to polish me, so I can see how I shine– and that, in fact, I do shine. That shine has always been in me. I just needed to believe I had it.

Obstacles in life can lay out like stepping-stones. Since they show up no matter what, why not use them differently? Use them in a way that works for you. Go for it; turn that stone over and look underneath! Be curious about what you once thought was just there to trip up your feet! A hindrance, you say. Learn to tell yourself that it's okay. In the bigger scheme of things, that slow down, or obstruction will serve you. Believe that. Give yourself the chance to believe that. We've already spent a lot of our time pondering otherwise, suffering through it. Remember the other side of the struggle. Visit that side. When you spot a bump on your road, feel excited at what you'll learn.

"Do not conform to the pattern of this world but be transformed by the renewing of your mind."
–Romans 12:2 NIV

Dealing with life, especially the tougher days, seems to be universal. We may suffer for quite a long time as we move slowly through the growth process. Sometimes, we go slower than necessary. Life is moving faster than we are, and we're falling behind. Conformity no longer feels pleasant. Better days don't know how to make their way to us. We're offered no new material to think from. No optional route. No transformation is happening.

Old, worn-out thoughts– perhaps about not having enough money to make ends meet or some other worry. I used to say shit like, "I'm always broke!" And yep, I always was. I felt that money was short most of the time; paydays were a bit of an exception, but otherwise, I steadily felt broke. I believed my feelings were justified when I saw my bank account figures or had to say no to buying certain things. It looked like I was broke, so I felt broke. And the more I felt broke, the more things showed up to justify and feed that feeling. I felt like I had no money, my thoughts said things to support the feeling and there I went and played it out every day. So subtle a move, yet so hypnotizing in its repetitive nature.

I've got to do something to change my mood, I thought. I need to go beyond whatever thoughts I had that made me feel low. I saw it was time for transformation to take its rightful place. The prefix "trans" means, "across" or "beyond". Of course it does.

I was looking out of the same window of the house, not realizing a different pleasing view was available. Such a con. Conformity doesn't move beyond the view it has. All that shit that I didn't really feel ownership for, conformity bought into. This made sense. Just the thought of it made so much sense to me.

Oh wow, from this angle...

Nothing like good ol' life experiences teaching us. Because, let's face it, they are doing that all the time. Whether we catch the lesson or not, the lesson is still there. Life is just that, a whole bunch of experiences stretched out like a movie reel. Some scenes are better than others. A few explosive scenes to stir things up and catch the viewer's eye. Life throws in some fireworks or struggles— however you want to see it. And that right there is hugely important!

How do you see it? And then what do you do? I never had the thought that I was being my own enemy, so I couldn't say that I was against me. It's in hindsight that I see who was behind the movie set of my life. Always me sitting in the director's chair, directing a low-budget film. I had low-budget ideas, so a low-budget life was what I was producing.

Oh, how that pissed me off— me as the enemy! But being mad at myself had to happen, or else I'd still be stuck in a depressive state. The back-and-forth wasn't my thing for long. The person I am today has acquired a lot of good life knowledge. I can go into my memory bank and pick experiences if I feel there is something there to learn, to implement, to heal from. So, go ahead and get mad, blow a little steam off if that's what it's going to take to clear your vision.

Do you really believe that?

I believe in really believing in yourself, and believing that you can most definitely accomplish what you feel called to do— and being called to live better is within all of us. That feeling grows so much that we can't hold it back. It's with me and with you at every turn. At some point, some of us will just go with it, giving in and trusting that direction pointing us inward toward "self". It's the self that is more than the person you see in the mirror, more than the storyline that person lives. It's the *you* who is invisible and running the show— the *you* who got you here, sustains you here and will call you to where you need to go. It's an ever moving presence, an energy force. I believe in that; it is easy to conclude that it makes total sense to believe in myself when my "self" is bigger than what my human eyes can see.

> "if you stand before others and are willing
> to say you believe in me, then I will tell my
> Father in heaven that you belong to me."
> —Matthew 10:32 ERV

When I read this for the first time, I took the message as is, *I say this, Jesus then tells God the Father about it and everything's good,* I would tell myself. And what I've come to reason now is so far from that simple understanding of mine. *In learning we evolve, in evolving we learn and in all of it, we grow. Choose to do it though.* This is what I've told myself and this is my newfound understanding of Matthew 10:32.

If that image I hold of myself, that image in my mind's eye, is something I can really feel into, that's when I "believe in myself". That's when my firm belief confirms that those images presented to my mind, that they belong here in the physical, where I can see, smell, touch, taste and hear them. They have life in my body, they've been seen in mind, now they just have to jump out onto the big screen of life. The images can take shape when I don't doubt that I can experience them beyond imagination, therefore I aim to gather the best images in mind.

Barbie commercials encourage young girls with the statement, "If you can see her, you can be her". The importance of seeing yourself as what you wish to experience. Use your mind to see yourself doing wonderful things, if that's your choosing. Seeing yourself in an enjoyable way is a much better use of your time, really. Try it. How will you pump yourself up and lead yourself if you haven't the faintest idea of what that version of you looks like? That version has a way of feeling, acting, talking, living life. Begin to play with that idea of seeing your ideal self roll through life being a boss. It's soothing. Like they say, there's nothing in imagination that is limited, unless you yourself create that limit. Every piece of material is there, every opportunity to get a different picture going. It's a secret garden that has always been there, awaiting your entry. Go on in. Just do it.

Take the time to go for it. Nike went for it and look

at the company now! Their motto still inspires athletes everywhere– and it's a good motto. There's a certain feeling that comes with each picture of yourself doing something. Test-driving your imagination includes getting to feel it out. I see mine, and I feel it. No one else gets to. I know that I feel good. My mind is filled with better images, ones that please me. I move as I choose, feeling my very best with each movement.

I know my mind is busy doing what it does: thinking, pondering, seeing images, replaying words– it does a lot. I now understand that it also needs an outlet, where it can release all the energies generated by the work it does every day. I see that me playing my role as a human is vital to my enjoyment here. I can't say there's an ideal age where one should be aware of one's participation, but from my personal experience it's been a blessing. I want to know how best to play my role. I understand the *how* of it all will just come naturally. I'll choose how to feel most of the time, so I can behave my best. "How" this or that will take place will simply fill in. What's going on at the command center is where it really all begins. Feel great, see great. Feel your very best as much as you can! Let that be where you spend most of your time.

UNMASK IT ALL

CHAPTER 1

Words sting

Oooh, those powerful words!

In seeking to understand myself more I could clearly see the pressure I had been under—or at least the pressure I had felt. It was as if the chips had been stacked up against me. My parents didn't really want me to be another addition to the family; they had their own beliefs and fears. I walked into a family that had pre-established rules for me, and premade ideas about my life; a mold had already been created, and I began to feel that I didn't quite fit into it. I tried and tried. The more I did, the more distant I felt.

I read somewhere, recently, that the deepest of feelings often cannot be described in words. I totally get that. But you most definitely feel them. Take love for instance. Love, real love, is felt. It shows itself in actions. Up until I understood language, I felt loved by my family. They made me laugh, which was fun. Up until I understood language, I felt some inclusion by my family, maybe even loved. Once my ears were able to translate speech it was as if the words counteracted or canceled out the actions.

As I glance at my childhood, I take myself right back to old feelings that left their mark on me. I think about the words that carried so much weight. Words that went in and made themselves at home, as if a part of me. Little comments, being made fun of, that was the worst. On one hand they wanted me to dress girly and when my mom dressed me up, they'd laugh at how I looked. They'd make fun of my hair (bowl cut/football helmet), my shoes, my socks (oversized ruffles), pretty much all of it. I felt disliked and unloved. And still, not safe enough to share.

Being so young, I thought from that youthful, vulnerable place. I only understood and reasoned from there. I was only a child. The impact of the commentary was strong. It seems that a child would opt for what seems easier, unaware of the pain it'll cause and leave behind.

What you got in your cup there?

"...For the mouth speaks what the heart is full of."
—Matthew 12:34 NIV

"For the word of God is living and active,
sharper than any double-edged sword..."
—Hebrews 4:12 ISV

I recall one day when we were out working, picking table grapes, I overheard my mother talking to a friend of hers. I think I was about eight years old. It was well over

100 degrees outside, and I was lying down in the back seat of our station wagon, which was parked under a large shade tree. I felt exhausted from the draining heat. My mother's friend seemed to be on a rampage asking my mom a series of questions which all centered around me. Why was I so lazy and defiant? Why did I act like a boy? How come I didn't work harder? So not only was I lazy, now I was a bad-mouthed little tomboy! I remember feeling like shit. I mean this was how they saw me and it didn't feel good at all. I was really interested in what my mother was about to say. But was I ready for it?

Time seemed to move so slowly as I intently listened to my mother's response. She went on to say that she herself didn't quite understand what was "wrong with" me, why I usually pushed back so much and why I did minimal work and chores around the house. Something was wrong with *me*? Wow. That hurt a whole lot. I just wanted to melt into the seat and disappear. I felt so alone, I didn't know how to take what I had just heard. Where could I run? Where could I hide? I was such a bother, why was I even here?

Fuck! How words alone can carry such importance, so much that your body has a reaction to it! Words and their definitions. We know they are more than just words; they express feelings and mindsets, views and perspectives. They feel loaded and land hella' heavy. Those words that day penetrated me in a way that made me feel helpless. Perhaps this was the first of many lessons that I would teach myself; that I had a world of my own to tend to. My face was being gently turned to look inward, although it felt more like a slap.

The spoken words of my parents and their colleagues, a glimpse of the ideas and beliefs of the people whose opinions I'd valued...I couldn't believe what they harbored. A critical mind spews critical words. I was young. I was a clean canvas, on which their words were splashed and painted, dark brush strokes drying slowly over what was beneath them. I was being covered up. Why did their words affect me so much? What happened to the saying, "Sticks and stones may break my bones, but words will never hurt me"? I guess I'd have to learn to make that true for myself. I really wanted to own that saying at some point in my life.

Out of the overflow of your heart, your mouth will speak what you hold inside, what you truly feel. Thinking about this scripture floods my mind with images—memories of my mother critiquing me for not acting like a girl. I remember all the words that scolded me and reminded me that I needed to behave according to other people's expectations and what other people were comfortable with. Those words sliced and diced at my heart.

The Bible refers to the tongue as a double-edged sword that can be used to lift someone up or tear someone down. That became painfully true for me. On one hand the words of my parents and their friends sure felt hurtful; and yet the phrase "words will never hurt me" rejects the idea of words being able to cause injury. The possibility of words not hurting me anymore was so soothing and refreshing to think about. Could I steel myself against them? Could my own kind words to myself overpower them? There was the double-edged sword explaining itself in the real live production of my life.

~

Whatchu thinkin' about? What you be saying?

"...Think of things that are excellent
and worthy of praise."
–Phillipians 4:8 NLT

"Be careful what you think, because
your thoughts run your life."
–Proverbs 4:23 NCV

"Girl, you can't just go around ignoring shit and living in la-la land!" I've heard this a million times. I used to say it too. That la-la land sounded way more fun though than facing reality sometimes. When I got my first professional job with Child Protective Services, I met a few people who meditated, practiced self-healing and believed in something bigger than human life such as: God, Creator, Source–something. They seemed truly happy and peaceful, and I wanted that vibe. The essence they gave off was intriguing. Something inside me knew it and my whole body felt it. There was a magnetism to their being. I wondered about what vibe I was giving off. What was habitually going on in my head? What kept showing up?

Was I thinking of excellent things, things worthy of praise? What thoughts were running the show? The discomfort of revealing them was immediate, but had a soothing effect, too, that would be ongoing.

Your attention is fuel; use it wisely and don't burn yourself.

I felt a bit embarrassed when I confronted my thoughts and the conversations going on within me. It sucks to feel the sting of self-trauma; but feeling it all the way out, was the only way to heal it. And what helps heal that trauma? You. *Self-help* as an entire section at the bookstore reads. It only made sense that this was where I ended up one day while at Barnes & Noble.

When it comes to picking out books and stationery cards I usually spot "the one" right away and stick with it. Gut feeling doing its job again. And this time it was the book A Bug Free Mind, by Andy Shaw. Imagine that: a mind full of bugs. Or better yet, imagine a mind that is free from bugs. I liked the idea of the second notion. My mind free of whatever was "bugging" it–yeah, I liked the sound of that.

Mr. Shaw's words explained so much, by carefully dissecting everyday conversations most of us engage in that are loaded with bugs. The conversations he spoke of were what we want to call innocent chats. The kind that invites us to tell the same story over and over and over. And the story we usually choose is one of self-defeat. We mean no harm by sharing our hurts and struggles. But in the innocence of wanting to be heard, we don't realize we're just adding another log to the fire that consumes us. Our fixed attention fuels it all. I truly felt his words. My mind did indeed have some bugs in it. His detailed explanation was encouraging.

Happy hour is one of those places where the *bug mind* spreads. Like misery loving its company. "Girl did you hear about my man cheating on me?" "What?" "Yes girl, just like Anna's man did to her!" "Omg, I think my husband is cheating too!" And the shared emotions of betrayal gain momentum. Sharing for upliftment and common understanding is one thing, but if not closely monitored is just calling for the bugs to move in and run the show!

As much as I don't like to hit the replay button on the self-bullying words that used to play in my head, it's a liberating step. Simple acts of "hanging out" to chit chat leads to heavy conversations stemming from heavy emotions.

Those words and thoughts connect to specific moments of my life; they all seem to fit together, as dysfunctional as they may be. It's important to ask yourself, more often than not: "Did you hear that?". With so many voices running through my mind at any given time, I started to pay attention to the ones that were the loudest. No surprise, the haters sat in the front row, heckling at every chance they got.

Hater talk says, "I'm so stupid for doing that." "What the hell was I thinking? I'm so dumb." "OMG, there I go again; I will never learn." "I look so ugly today.", "I'm always broke!" "Fuck my life!" "I've always been the black sheep."

That's just some of what I call the haterism speech that ran through my mind before. Why did I do this to myself? I'd never asked myself that question. It's as if I'd been convinced that those thoughts were true. Why resist them? It felt so hopeless. Those negative, self-defeating comments were strewn all over my mind. I had an infestation going on. There were too many of those fuckers in there. Ugh! No wonder I exploded so often.

The thoughts that float in our minds—the ones that go against our own selves—they've got to go. Carefully and lovingly seeing them for what they are helped me build the bridge I used to cross from my thoughts to my life. My life and my thoughts. Inseparable, I know now. With that being said, I told myself, "Inside I shall fearlessly continue to go and know." Jumping into full enthusiastic interest, that's exactly what you want to go for!

CHAPTER 2

Deep Divin'

Why hello—come on in!

"The ancestor of every action is a thought."
—Emerson

I just want to be digestible enough to my family, so they'll see past my flaw (what I used to think about my sexual orientation) is what I thought as I stood with my hands on my hips looking back and forth at the clothes in my closet. None of it seemed feminine enough for the family to approve. Granted I didn't really want to wear what they wanted but I didn't want to ruffle anymore feathers or answer the question 'Why aren't you wearing a dress or a skirt?'. We all knew why, so that question was insulting to say the least. I decided to go see what I had in my dresser, and it didn't help. As I pulled out the bottom drawer, jeans and Dickies pants, of course. I went on to open the next drawer, full of t-shirts and tank tops, made sense. And I knew the top drawer wouldn't help with it being undergarments, so I scratched my head, took a deep breath and plopped myself at the foot of my bed. I placed my hands underneath my thighs and stared at the floor. I told myself I didn't want to spend money on clothes I didn't like. And the reality of showing up with jeans would require at least the top to be *girly*. Every thought directed itself at appeasing the family. And many of the acts performed by me going forward stemmed from these self-denying thoughts.

Inside. The part of me that holds all the questions and answers. It is said that for every question there is an answer, and for every answer there is a question. One is made for the other. Inside my memory bank, where all of my life's experiences remain, I have my very own Q & A spot. I have memories of all my experiences too. I noticed some more than others—the ones that stung and left scars. I've learned that feelings have their own rules of conduct. Sad, happy, angry, calm... every emotion I have is tied to different scenes of my life. It's kind of trippy to see my mind taking me down different corridors of myself. And we think we know ourselves so well. Just give your mind a chance to show you what you're really holding onto.

In my mind I saw what looked like a mansion with many rooms, each housing experiences connected to specific emotions. As I walked down the halls and corridors of my mind, I smiled, laughed, cried, pondered and reflected. So, so many rooms, all occupied— many by painful experiences. My mansion felt sad. It sure wasn't Hearst Castle or anything from a fairy tale (*well maybe Beauty and the Beast, right before the beast turned human again*). I wasn't too sure I wanted to continue this mind journey, all of my former experiences glancing at me as I walked by. I could feel the love some of them held, so this propelled me to continue moving through. I owed myself this much.

Dusting off the old imagination.

"Imagination is the beginning of creation. You imagine what you desire, you will what you imagine and at last you create what you will."
–George Bernard Shaw

I was interested in creating a new way for my life, but imagination seemed like child's play and very fairytale oriented. I'll be honest: I felt it was a waste of my precious time. But you know, all those books I read had addressed it and encouraged it. They woke me up to the idea that we are already imagining tons of things. And a lot of them are so random. The imagination is happening, but we're often asleep at the wheel and missing it.

Walt Disney held the vision of Disneyland in his mind. He saw an open field, but he also saw the finished product. He was able to hold his vision to the one in his mind. As I walked by my living room tv, I heard these statements. I was in the middle of doing laundry and would often have the tv on in case something good came on (or maybe as an excuse to sit down for a sec). I stopped and stood right in front of the tv and listened. The talk about Disneyland being created from the images Walt had in his mind was intriguing. I found myself with my head tilted in fascination. *If Walt can create Disneyland, fuck, why can't I create a better life, I totally can. Imagination huh, ok, I'd down.*

Given all of that, I decided that someone needed to step up and dictate how things were gonna' go down from now on. I was beginning to believe that my mind was blindly running my life, the decisions I made, how I felt most of the time and what I expected to happen. This time I was going to participate– blinders off! Excitedly, my imagination went to work. I pictured a blank black space. I pictured a large rectangular desk, shimmering in white light; like the sidewalk squares that light up on the music video Billy Jean. I saw myself playing all the roles. I was the one sitting behind the desk as the CEO of my domain. I saw two muscular bodyguards at each end of the desk as well. I felt powerful there. I established a waiting room, so that the former versions of me could come out of their rooms and know that I was ready to talk with and to honor them.

I knew that I felt heavy within due to all the "holding on" I was doing– holding on to hurt, rejection, sadness, hopelessness and fear. I no longer wanted the hurt to be my only story; I knew that it was part of it, but not all of it. The moment had come to have some difficult talks with myself. The space in my mind felt cleansed and said, "bring it on". With a cup of coffee in hand I joyfully began.

Captain, I'm going in!

When I began to call up the experiences that I had shoved away, those that I'd never wanted to encounter again, I was pleasantly surprised at how doable it felt. A restorative process was well underway.

I was drawn to a room far in the back of my mind, a

very small room holding five-year-old me's experiences. There was a tug that I just couldn't ignore. That five-year-old had been given a heavy load. She was so young and innocent and yet she carried on as best she could.

The little girl inside this room was surrounded by playful cats and kittens, she had a smile on her face as she stroked a large orange cat that was on her lap. She giggled at the playfulness of the kittens around her. I could feel that their love was just enough to penetrate her already hardened shell. I was thankful that love was at her side and knew just how to reach her, even though she may not have been aware of what it was. It felt good for me to know this, it made me feel ecstatic that she was indeed loved so much. The room had an energy about it, a heaviness. I couldn't understand why if I was observing such happy moments.

I stepped through the door and she immediately got up and ran to me and held on tight. I welcomed it. We both cried tears of relief and joy. There was so much love flowing between us. She felt validated and rescued. She was excited to be reunited, to catch up with where life had taken her. She'd waited for so long. We both had. A sense of relief was present as I grabbed her hand. We both smiled as we walked past the many rooms she had never seen before. I knew I had isolated her. I felt I had not given her a fair chance at being her true authentic self. But I also knew that I was extremely appreciative for the perseverance she had demonstrated.

I said, "Hey little you, I love you. Know that I am in awe at all that you took in. I still remember your likes and dislikes, I'm still unraveling your gifts. Your nature of innocence has never left me, so thank you. Thank you for doing the best you could with what you knew then.

Thank you for holding that place for us, for being the trooper that you were. Thank you for it all. And by the way, cats are still with us, doing their thang! Those love tokens you kept sending me— every single one has been fervently appreciated.'

All I could see was the beautiful smile on her face and the excitement at being drawn out of that room that I held her in for so long. I did not sense any anger or ill will emanating from her, but rather sheer joy that we were together. At last, I had made my way inside. I had shown myself that I could be courageous enough to recover my childlike faith. From there, I would come to understand the importance of uniting all of me.

Ah, now I see. It has always been me. I've been in the driver's seat, but feeling like I've been in the trunk— out of place, out of control, in the dark, uncomfortable within myself. You been there, too? Even though it's all on the inside, you point out everything outside yourself, all the circumstances that made you act in a certain way. "It's all their fault," you might have said, over and over.

Looking deeply into these circumstances and experience can expose the mindset that fueled the bad feelings. In a powerfully silent way, your past and current thoughts will come together and take a harmonious center stage in your life. See what's behind the curtain. And don't be surprised when your understanding shifts. When you feel like life is serving you more wins, big or small, but nonetheless you know you're winning now.

CHAPTER 3

Mad winning now!

Anger: Use it wisely.

> "Anger cannot be dishonest."
> —Marcus Aurelius, Meditations

The Bible says that anger in and of itself is not bad; it's rather what you do with that anger. Jesus tossed over the tables of the merchants in the market. He hurt no one when he did that. But got the attention of the crowd. That kind of anger is just like a slap on the face when you need to wake up and see things for what they are. Anger can motivate. I've felt it at times when I've found myself in a situation that was all too familiar, and I've thought "fuck, not again." I've found myself struggling down the bumpy road that I swore I would avoid.

I may be down a similar road, but this time, I must remind myself the road has many exits and detours. I can choose to let this road lead me differently. I'm never too far down any road that I can't navigate myself back on track. I must remember that. As that familiar anger finds its place within me, it has another purpose to serve– and that is to shake me up to wake me up.

The huge surge of energy that accompanies that feeling, like tremors shaking the ground, sure gets our attention. This anger is in a category all its own; it's the friendly type, because it's really personal. It seeks to be used on oneself for the betterment of oneself. So, we exclaim, "That's it! I am done with this...aaahhhh!!! I'm so fucking mad. I'm gonna' do things differently!". Anger acknowledges it has hit the mark and you have responded accordingly. Anger has served you.

This fiery little emotion has freed so many of us. Toxic and harmful relationships end when this anger hits you. New doors to jobs are opened when this anger propels you to seek more. Confidence finds its rightful place within you when this anger teaches you how to laugh at thinking any less of yourself. The moments leading up to the bang are not so pleasant, for sure. There may well be an outlet along the way, but I'm sure we can all agree that we've passed a lot of those by, which has led to the burst(s) of anger.

When you are angry, you experience physical and emotional pain. Anger strongly motivates you to do something about it. And when you take action, it calms your "nerves." That's why you may have an angry reaction and then feel so calm afterward; your energy has been spent and then restored.

Turn anger in your favor. Feeling a little angry from time to time will remind us all to look for the rest stops that are strewn all along the way. We don't always have to look at anger as only "bad." When it shows up, sometimes it really is there to help, sort of like a mega rest stop that refreshes you and sends you back on the road ready to go! Baby, it's demo time!

Demolition time.

Watching a building explode, on purpose, is pretty breathtaking– exciting, even. There's a plan already in place, for change, for something new. So, boom, there goes the old construct. Can a person explode, on purpose? Can we explode in a way in which we are deciding to do it? Not from a heat-of-the moment reaction, where we feel embarrassed for our rash behavior, but intentionally? I say absolutely yes. Go for a hike and scream at the top of your lungs if you feel "fed up" with anything.

Write down all your worries, frustrations, concerns, and questions. Then read them aloud And burn that shit. Explode in a release of all the heavy weights. Explode.

Let the inside of you burst open and unleash the "enough is enough" aspects of your life. Choose to explode in such a way that pleases you, hurting no one and feeling like a million bucks through the whole process (which is all your own). Think about what feelings you want to house inside of yourself. Sometimes you've got to explode a little to make room for your own self. After all, you pay all the bills via the emotions you must take on and feel. Therefore, embrace the change that awaits to be invited into your life. Give it a shot!

The one-two change up!

Five points against my driving record. Five points! The night replayed in my head. My car smelled like Taco Bell as I waited for the red light to change. Oh shit, now I'm awake and realize my hands aren't on the steering wheel and I'm bouncing all over the place. I'm being tossed around as my car is mowing down the plants on the center divider and then bam! The right side of my rib cage was slammed by the center console while the seat belt across my chest and legs gashed my skin open. As I coughed from the air bag particles, my bones ached immediately. No getting out of this one. I sat there confused and ashamed. The pain from the crash was slowly reaching my body. I have no idea how long I sat there, but I quickly heard sirens and could see the red and blue lights from the police cars. *Fuck dude, how could you let this happen?* My mind was so quick to judge, to critique, to insult, to ridicule. Granted as I was asked to perform the DUI and breathalyzer test, I was hoping that the nightmare would end, and I would just wake up shitting my pants from a horrific dream. Yeah, I much rather have shitted my pants in bed than to have to imagine what I'd be dealing with from this accident.

As I sat on the curb of the sidewalk, trying to keep warm, a police officer approached me and told me that my blood alcohol level was .05% but that he smelled marijuana in the car, so he asked if I had been smoking. I don't know if the cold morning air affected my rational thinking, but I said that yes, I'd been smoking. Why the hell did I do that? Well, that explains why I got hit with a wet reckless charge. In the State of California this is considered a charge reduction, carrying less punishment than a DUI. That didn't matter to me, I felt like an idiot. DUI or wet reckless, they both screamed embarrassment. *I so wish this didn't happen*, I silently exclaimed. In hindsight, this episode served tenfold. Never ever do we want the lesson if it comes with pain. But dammit we'll be sure to be first in line to get the gain.

We all have said at one time or another, "I wish that wouldn't have happened," or "I wish I would've never done X-Y-Z." I stop to think about events in my life and who I was in that moment. From where I stand now, I can see the gradual change in myself. As more hurtful experiences occurred in my life, I did change. The change could've gone either way. But for me, it was wonderful. I started grasping life and enjoying it more and more– including the stupid-ass shit that had happened. Once I could see just how much smarter I became after going through the struggle, it planted the idea of that moment being "epic" for me. A mark on the trail of my life. Each struggle then became a mark on the trail of my life. A mark that meant something. It meant growth and maturity.

I totally get that experiences leave an emotional impact. But the impact can be used in whichever way we choose. We can believe it has crippled us and that it is the reason our life is so miserable. Or we can believe it happened to wake us up to the idea that we can live better. I can see situations differently now because I stand in a different place. I understand more and am willing to argue less. I choose to look at what was there that I didn't see before, regardless of whether it was because I was stubborn or just naive.

The value factor of the tougher days never expires. There's always an opportunity for a new mindset, a new perspective. Standing on the level of interest for comprehension's sake, the air feels refreshing and inviting. The problem looks different. It seems favorable. Like advice from a friend that I feel in my bones.

The common thread that I know of in my life, the one I can do anything with, is me. Accepting my participation in all the events of my life, owning up, is not the easiest task, but it does reap a multitude of rewards. Finding the "aha moment" in any struggle, past or present, is priceless.

A Filled Life vs. a Full Life

"Joyful is the person who finds wisdom,
the one who gains understanding."
–Proverbs 3:13 NLT

I like to read a lot; I find myself reading books, articles, blogs and even quotes written on street walls. I'm not 100 percent sure where I picked up the idea of "living a filled life versus a full life", but it got my attention and felt worth exploring. It also felt like a safe statement to make, not too loaded and truthful to some degree. I remember hearing some people say that they'd had "a good, full life." I assume that whatever filled their life to capacity was to their liking. I think it must be similar to feeling a full belly; whatever food went in must've been really enjoyable. But just like no matter how much we eat, we will eventually get hungry again, in life, we'll eventually need more to keep the tank filled. Some of us will need to empty the tank of all the pollutants that have settled in, before we can fill up at all.

Full, means "containing a lot" and is used to describe a container that has reached its maximum capacity. Filled, means to "make or become full" and is used when talking about putting something in a container. Having a cup full of goodness is great. Having a cup that is poured into continuously is awesome, if what's poured in is healthy.

Our cups have been poured into it since childhood. For some of us, our minds are full of beliefs, ideas and memories that no longer jive with who we currently are; we have reached our limit of what we can hold of them. And we can't replace them without first emptying them out. We can't fill something that is already full.

When there's movement in a stream or a river, your eyes can see it is being filled from something greater. You see the water moving, crashing against rocks, steadily flowing forward, making its way regardless of the path. You may see small whirlpools off to the side, usually in a smaller pool surrounded by larger rocks. The water there is going in circles, collecting leaves, sticks, and anything else that isn't flowing. It's sort of sidelined– still part of the stream, but just spinning going nowhere.

Both images always remind me of me– of us as humans. Sometimes we're holding on to stuff that hurts, letting ourselves be full of it, to justify our behavior or personality. Other times we spin around inside the problem, creating a whirlpool that sucks us in. We remove ourselves from believing better and differently. We choose to remain full.

Yep, we are too full. The past that we were meant to learn from and move beyond has our mind full. We're in our own world, going in circles over the same shit from the past. The sun rises to begin a new day, and yet we feel the exact same way we did days or weeks or even years ago. Every now and then, we join the flow of joy, but we're quick to sideline. The pull of repetitive safe behavior is far more attractive to some of us and there we go, off track.

Picturing myself as both makes sense. I feel a lot of relief in knowing I can see it all much more clearly now. I'm staying in a flow state these days. I'm welcoming in life as it's happening, filling up my cup with what I like and enjoy, and gently rolling down the stream.

My suggestion to you with these analogies is to be gentle with yourself if you do see yourself sidelined or spinning in that whirlpool. Seeing it that way makes it silly yet provides the gentle nudge for you to pay attention to where you are. It's too easy to veer off track and stay off track. A pit stop can always be useful and refreshing but too many of them will prolong your journey.

Stay open to new ideas, new perspectives, new information about what interests you. This way you remain available to be filled with the things of your choosing. Remaining stuck in old ways, such as negative self-talk keeps your mind full. Empty the contents by writing them out, one by one. You might know what I'm about to suggest next. Yes, read that statement aloud. Laugh at the statement, cry, release whatever emotion that naturally comes up for you and then crumple up the paper and pretend to be Steph Curry and shoot a 3 pointer with it, right into your wastebasket.

THE LOVE WAVE

CHAPTER 1

Confusing, messy...love?

Love via actions. Love without a word.

> "Love is patient, love is kind. It does not envy,
> it does not boast, it is not proud. It does not
> dishonor others, it is not self-seeking, it is not
> easily angered, it keeps no record of wrongs.
> Love does not delight in evil but rejoices with
> the truth. It always protects, always trusts,
> always hopes, always perseveres."
> –1 Corinthians 13:4-7 NIV

Animals don't speak our language, and yet we know they love us. How do we know? We say it's because we can feel it. Show it, display it– that's how you really say it!

Rev up the engines of love and then shift them into drive. Love will lead you to places of profound peace and tranquility. The love we already have within us is a bubbling brook. More than enough for us to share. I am never truly emptied now, just not always filled. And this filling? Who is responsible?

As a child I never held anyone responsible for loving me. I had no concept of love then. I would come to know when I either felt good or not, but the idea of love was not even on my mind. As young children none of us really knows– but our soul does. The "feeling good or not" is an early indicator. Being yelled at doesn't feel good. Being shoved and hit doesn't feel good. Hearing words that say you're less-than– they don't feel good either. All these things that hurt seem to surround us. With our eyes wide open we see things that don't feel good to look at. Our senses pick it all up. Smells of deteriorating homes, cities. Sounds of violence and hatred. All five senses pick up on everything that is coming out of other human beings.

So, there it is, all of it, the good and the bad, all out in the world. It's all floating around, no matter where we go, and we place things in one of the two categories– we make two piles– good or bad.

It's fascinating to realize that we each can interpret the same thing quite differently. Some of us are sensitive to other people's words, while others aren't phased by them. Some of us have built walls, while others don't feel the need for those walls. Perhaps their upbringing taught them differently. I would say it's during childhood when we begin to shape our unique perspectives.

Think about a loving, supportive home versus a home filled with domestic violence and negative talk. The vibes in those two settings are so different. The thing is two people can even be in the same environment and give very different accounts of what went on. How could that be? Well, as I see it from my experience, our outer world that we shared was the same, while our individual inner worlds were not.

Laying down new bricks

Amid those early years here on Earth, we don't have any filters in place. We grow up where we grow up. We have the parents we have, siblings or not, and socioeconomic status already established before our arrival. Given that a foundation will have been laid for you before you were even born, you will have to work with that foundation as you move forward in life.

Sometimes the foundation was all fucked up from the beginning; you had no part in it at all. Everything you begin to believe firmly, the thoughts that point the way and say who you are, get built on that foundation. And then, you enter the latter years of young adulthood, and you not liking the person that you are. Now what? Well, you'll either stand by it regardless of the mess it is by saying things like, "I'm always gonna be this way!" or "I'm never gonna change!". Ideally, you will move through those thoughts and into a time where you recognize that you yourself are a fixer upper.

Look closely at the foundation of yourself. If you like some parts, then keep them. If you don't like any of who you are, then yay– go shopping mentally! Do whatever it takes in mind, to build yourself on a foundation of your choosing.

Ask simple questions like, "How do I feel right here, right now?". Answer honestly and be gentle with whatever your answer is. That question establishes to yourself that you care about you. It's a starting point.

What excites you? You, not others or your kids or partner. Do you do any of those things? These questions reveal what is at the core of how we live, how we think, believe or not believe. They are your foundation. Figure out if the foundation is what feels true to you?

For example, when I was young I was very embarrassed of my arms because they were hairy, and I mean hairy! I felt ugly because of them. Over the years I lived with the jokes, stares and side eyeing. Those hairy arms told me years ago that I was not pretty. I let the outside tell the inside what to think and feel. It began to settle until it formed as part of my foundational mind. That idea, false idea, has to go! New foundation is needed, one planted on love. Love is kind, end of story. In knowing that, experientially, I began to lay that down day by day.

If you think your parents screwed you over while you were growing up, just remember they had their own foundations. Maybe they never rebuilt or felt the need to. Yeah, our parents should be our heroes and provide a safe platform for us to walk onto, but sometimes it just isn't that way. I never really gave much thought to what my parents' childhoods were like. How were they treated by their own parents? What was the vibe in their homes growing up? Were my grandparents loving or harsh?

Did my parents decide to change anything about their upbringing? Their beliefs? Since they were my parents and I was learning from them, I never thought to question anything until life started to hurt. When the days are less enjoyable, you ask questions. They may not be the "aha"-questions, but you've got to start somewhere.

Do I love me?

I know now that love is the one thing that leads the way. Love shining a light, letting you see just enough to move in a direction of more clarity. We're not always aware, in the middle of our pain and deep thoughts, that love is behind the scenes. Love is in the background prompting us to ask questions that will lead to new questions. It happens little by little and that it happens at all is fucking awesome!

There was a mix of love and rejection in me for quite a while. The painful words and facial expressions that conveyed rejection were like a thundering storm around me. I was cared for by being served a warm meal every single day– yeah, in that way, there was love. I didn't know it was love then, but I knew that gesture felt a lot safer and kinder than the rest.

I had shelter, warm clothes and bedding, delicious food cooked up by my mother, entertainment provided by my siblings and many cats that sought me out. Love was proving itself through those actions. My parents never said the words, "I love you" to me. I never felt sad about it, though. I don't think I even gave it a second thought. It was as if something inside of me noticed, gathered that realization, and placed it somewhere safe where I could later retrieve it when ready.

With my own life and its movements, one thing kept creeping in– something I ignored, without really knowing I was ignoring it. This one beautiful missing piece, never really missing, just not activated, was self-love.

Getting myself to finally shed a light on this key component was as unique a journey for me as it is for everyone else. Loving myself has been and is what makes me smile. I don't have to ask anyone to do a single thing for me to feel this genuine love inside of myself. It's a love that has reshaped my life. It can do the same for you, changing everything from what you see to how you hear things. Love refines all that is necessary for you to live life in an enjoyable way, and it buffers out the rest.

My apology, my refreshment.

> "Forgiveness is the fragrance of the violet
> on the heel of the one who crushed it."
> —Mark Twain

Life takes on a much lighter feeling when love has taught you how to forgive others and yourself. Forgiveness can find its way into your heart when you least expect it; but you also must sometimes draw it in. You have to want the relief and the softness that comes from forgiving. After much practice, you learn that it benefits you as much as the one who hurt you. Your forgiving is as pleasant as a soft fragrance. The hurt led to you forgiving and that's just beautiful; forgiveness smells great on you.

Love forgives. It finds ways to make more room for itself. It is in a constant flowing motion, always at your side. When the days are darkest, and times are most difficult this idea may be far from our mind— and when it does enter our mind, it isn't able to last in such darkness. A little light goes a long way.

CHAPTER 2

Love is and isn't...

Glimmering light of love.

I've had so many people in my past who wanted to share with me their love for God, Jesus, the Creator, the Universe, Mother Earth, the All Knowing, something bigger than our humanity. They wanted to share with me how they found a relationship with themselves there that saved them and transformed their lives. Every time they spoke about who they used to be and how the love of this Being saved them, I felt how much they believed that. They had something special that sparkled in their eyes. Little did I know then that it was that spark of light, that little flame of love that was reaching out to me. The inner pilot flame, I call it, always ready to ignite us from within. The dark moments can be seen as helpers, like ushers guiding you to your rightful seat. Love makes all things seem more friendly.

So, why do we stand in the dark for longer than necessary? It doesn't make sense that we would choose to hurt ourselves for a prolonged period. What I mean by choosing to hurt ourselves is that sometimes we recognize that a situation isn't in our best interest, but we do nothing to change it. For example, take being in a toxic relationship, where perhaps you're verbally abused or even physically assaulted. You would know immediately that those actions were causing you to hurt, but yet you might choose to stay. Because of that choice, the darkness may remain a bit longer, until another light comes your way— another moment to choose, another opportunity to make a different choice powered by patience and love.

Self-love began to grow from the darkest of places within me. Self-love, like a seed, grand in and of itself, appearing so tiny and inconsequential. Do not let your eyes mislead you! See the great redwoods and the seeds they once were. Believe in that. Believe in the fact that love, as small as it may seem to start, has so much to do. Self and love must meet. The real self, the self that feels natural to you, has its own blueprint that it must follow to feel fulfilled. It's the same self that feels zapped when told that it is ugly or not special; is the self that has let go of love's hand. Love would never, ever accept those ideas. Love would not allow you to feel like shit. It only allows the pain from those words, so that you'll learn that they feel painful because they're not true.

Hanging on to painful words and experiences is common. I know firsthand. I did it for a long-ass time. When you feel your life sucks, you tend to write a story for yourself that supports all of the low notes of life. If it really sucks, you repeat the worst stories of betrayal and bad luck to match the suck factor. It's almost like relinquishing any say you have in how your life is rolling out. Now you've claimed yourself as a victim, and you're focused on getting the crowd to feel sorry for you. I highly doubt that love would advise me to set up a pity party. I love to party, and pity and party do not mix. (*I'd much rather replace the term "pity party" with "pity pit."*) And I remember that "love keeps no record of wrongs," so why should I?

Slowly observing what didn't feel like love was actually my way of taking mental notes. I may not have known I was doing it, but this again shows me how active love was during those times. Even as I slept at the wheel of my own life, love was steadily showing up every single day. I'd say it had perfect attendance!

Where is the love?

"There is no fear in love..."
−1 John 4:18 NIV

"I have often wondered how it is that every man loves himself more than all the rest of men, but yet sets less value on his own opinions of himself than on the opinions of others."
−Marcus Aurelius, Meditations

It was weird to think that I was being careless with my life and its many decisions, by not loving myself. That was the reason I always felt out of place or not relaxed. I was always looking around, suspicious and leery of life. I suppose looking just through the eyes of myself as Paula,

I was limited. Fear created a one-man show that I starred in. Life is awesome though, in that it uses everything, even the smallest things, to teach us, to reach us, to wake us up. Not loving myself was rock-bottom, but that was just the angle I needed to see what I was doing. Honestly, I can tell you that I realized then that I didn't really love myself as I'd thought I did. I guess that, up until then, it hadn't been obvious to me; if it had been I suppose I would've made some changes. But it was really my own thoughts about myself, my low self-esteem, and always thinking about the worst-case scenario. Throw in jealousy and timidness– distant relatives of fear, and not my best qualities. I swear I didn't want my mind to ponder that shit, but it did anyway.

There were days when I would talk out loud to God and ask questions. I felt lost and lonely. I wondered why I suffered. I asked what the purpose of my own existence was. I saw the days I was living through, and I wasn't happy with them overall.

When I caught myself in a good mood, it was like magic. I wanted that feeling to last forever. But it was always an up and down thing. I never really trusted in God, let alone myself. I asked for help and quickly abandoned ship if it was too hard for too long. How could I get any answers if I didn't stick around to hear them? I was always looking for something, always asking.

> "I looked in temples, churches and mosques.
> But I found the Divine within my heart."
> –Rumi

I searched and searched. I was convinced that a part of me was yet to be found. I would read my Bible as often as I could. I began when my ex-husband was incarcerated. He "found Jesus," as they say, in prison and shared his new-found relationship with me. It was very different for me to hear, but the scriptures were soothing and calming. The words I read really spoke to me. Even though there was a lot I didn't understand, I felt the need to keep reading it. It had an addictive nature to it; something in me really liked it. The words seemed to be alive and to carry a different energy within them. It was as if all of this I was now feeling had been inside of me all along.

Reading something you're not used to, and enjoying it so much that it trips you out, is the kind of thing you keep to yourself for a while. You kind of want to see where it leads. You don't want to look silly, you tell yourself. But you keep going with whatever new ideas are coming up— ideas that feel refreshing and leave the old, former ways feeling outdated. Taking your mind off of the fear factor, and resting on faith, creates a very different energy.

Fear was such a third wheel.

> "...perfect love drives out fear..."
> −1 John 4:18 NIV

Love isn't afraid to fail, afraid to make new friends at school, afraid to *make a fool* of itself, afraid to be unsuccessful, and on and on and on. It totally makes sense that love and fear don't mix. When I realized that I didn't have love for myself, at least not enough that would be sufficient to enjoy my days, I also realized that I was disrespecting God, the Creator, the very essence of my being and existence. If God created me and was the very breath that gave my body life every day, I should be nicer to that me. By being nice to myself, I was being nice to God who lived in me. My mind really chewed on this idea. If I love God, I have to love myself. If I don't love myself, then God is shunned, limited by fear.

Faith and fear, like oil and water, just don't mix. They show themselves to the naked eye as separate entities: they will not merge. Love encourages in so many ways; it feeds faith. The constant fear I had of rejection and of others' opinions of me... Love doesn't think like that! There is no fear in love. Fear never invites love, and vice versa. These two can't reside with one another. The fear itself was a sign that love wasn't my guiding light. I felt like a renter with a tenant who wouldn't leave. I needed to cast out the fear. Love was my strong arm.

When I didn't have love for myself, things in my life would seem to get out of control. My two long-term relationships dissolved into very toxic environments. The toxicity spilled over onto my children. They heard and saw behaviors that I'm not proud of. My lack of love for myself left room for me to seek love out there that could fill me, that could help me in some way.

When I got together with my children's father, I was seventeen years old— a senior in high school and rather tomboyish. I was really shy and somewhat of a nerd, which showed in my high academic achievements. I met him through my best friend; she was dating his cousin. Long story short, we hit it off right away. We both had a good sense of humor, both had our parents at home, were of Mexican heritage, and really enjoyed the outdoors. As young as I was, I knew that the time I shared with him made me feel an acceptance I hadn't quite felt before. I mean, this was a boy who was telling me he loved me—and his actions actually supported what he told me, so how could I question anything? I felt that he was giving me something I didn't have and hadn't experienced. He loved me for me and we had fun together. I may not have loved who I was, but he did. That was enough of a reason for me to stick around.

All that attention he was giving me felt wonderful. I was so young; I had no idea that I was placing a huge burden on him. I'm sure he had no understanding of the burden I was placing on him, either. I hadn't ever experienced this kind of love, and I didn't realize that over time I'd become addicted to it. I would feel that only he could validate me. He brought the love that I just couldn't conjure up for myself. Did I know that right then and there? No, of course not. Soon enough, though, I'd learn that he had placed the same kind of burden on me. We were mirroring each other, and, yet we both were blinded the entire time.

Knock, knock...help!

> "Why are you knocking at every other door?
> Go, knock at the door of your own heart."
> —Rumi

I can agree that when we met, we both saw the best in each other and therefore offered our best to the other. Our best was our best. We blindly knocked at each other's door, seeking from one another something we already had and just couldn't see; thus, the blinders.

Nothing against him or I, or our former selves, but our best at the time was like driving with a quarter of a tank. It's just enough to get you so far. When someone else is made responsible for keeping your tank full, whether you are aware of it or not, you'll only get so far. You don't realize how much time you'll spend on the side of the road, waiting for the next person to come by and fill you up a bit more. Then when they can't, you'll say they were the problem. Back to the side of the road you go.

Yeah, I know what that view looks like— standing there in my life, feeling empty as fuck, sad as fuck and wondering what the fuck! You probably know, too. You try new things; "Something has to give," you say to yourself. You change one small thing and wait for big changes. You change something else and look around: "Oh fuck it. I'm just gonna stay the same, nothing has changed, nothing works!" Hold on, now. Think about what you are changing. Is it something inside of you, or is it outside of you?

Should've checked my motives!

"What do you mean?" you ask. Well, to fix my self-esteem, I decided to work out. It didn't sound like such a bad idea. I wasn't overweight or advised of any health conditions, but I knew that exercising felt good and cleared my mind. Now enter a time when I worked out to "look good" so that it would be easier to date and find a partner. I joined a small boxing gym soon after I filed for divorce from my children's father, and I loved it. I was in the best shape of my life. I think I was about twenty-eight years old.

That little plan of mine to "look good" for the hook-up worked in a one-sided way. At the gym where I trained, I met my very first girlfriend. She was the only other female at that gym, and we often sparred together, so it was easy to chat and get to know each other. She had a girlfriend at the time, and of course I was freshly divorced. Over some months, our friendship grew, and we began to hang out. One thing led to another, and we soon became lovers. I, then, was perfectly fine with her having a girlfriend already; I wanted nothing to do with a committed relationship. The fact that she was already with someone was perfect— not dealing with a partner sounded like music to my ears. The "looking good" part of working out had accomplished its mission. I had taken care of the exterior, my looks, and had confirmation of it from my *friend with benefits*.

The entire time, mutual feelings were growing for one another. We had no idea what we really were like. We only knew each other as lovers at this point. We offered the best of each other and again, I only had so much in my tank. And I didn't know what her reserves were. I found myself in a mess. There was an attraction, and it had come from an unhealthy place. Parts of us cry out to us. The cry is internal, so that only we can hear it. The volume of the cry depends on how far we find ourselves from ourselves. Some of us will move great lengths to regain our balance.

"It is good to grasp the one and not let go of the other. Whoever fears God will avoid all extremes."
–Ecclesiastes 7:18 NIV

Now I understand this scripture about avoiding extremes. Extreme means, going to great or exaggerated lengths (Merriam- Webster), I went to the extreme of choosing to put my physical looks above my actual feelings. I suppose it just seemed a lot easier to cheat a little and make a change to my body, where I could see actual results, than to change my mind or my spirit. I could easily hide my feelings, so for the most part, no one knew a thing.

What's funny is that I was really and truly cheating myself, because the feelings I had were still there. Those little guys didn't get worked out at all. And that is exactly what happens when you go to an extreme: the other side gets neglected. Remember, you have to keep your balance. You must play both sides.

CHAPTER 3

Quiet, beautiful love.

That Day.

> "I wait with silent passion for one
> gesture, one glance from you."
> —Rumi, The Love Poems of Rumi

There I was, washing my hands in the warm water. I had the day off from work and was feeling chill. I remember staring at myself in the mirror for a lot longer than I'd ever done. This time it wasn't just for personal hygiene. My eyes caught my attention. I felt frozen for a while. I don't even remember blinking. I remember smiling so much that my cheeks began to hurt. I couldn't pull away from my own gaze; it felt magnetic. I was drawn in, and yet I felt shy at the same time. I felt something inside of me stirring up. A surge of tears started running down my face, they felt hot, like they were springing up from a volcano deep inside of me.

I wasn't really comprehending what was going on, but it felt cleansing and warm. I felt loved and sad at the same time. Sad that I hadn't loved myself correctly or sufficiently. Sad that I had basically begged for love in the past through the harmful actions I'd taken. I felt like I'd disrespected myself so much. And yet I felt loved in this moment. Just experiencing it made me able to feel the love that is always present and available to me. I wanted to keep this going! I knew I had to continue to figure out the best ways to love myself– to live in such a way that I'd know, beyond a shadow of doubt, that I loved myself. I welcomed and embraced my blossoming. Better yet, I understood that it had to take place. So as I stood there crying, I began to talk to myself out loud. I asked myself for forgiveness and I forgave. I told myself how much I adored and valued myself and I really felt those words, like fresh water to parched lips. I opened the floodgates of my heart and poured it out onto myself. It felt sort of awkward at first, but I knew I deserved to hear it, I also deserved to say it and to watch myself do so. I was all in.

When I recall that day, I still cry. I still feel that immense love that engulfed me, the love that was and is never far away. It's truly amazing that this much love existed in me all along.

> "You have within you more love
> than you can understand."
> –Rumi

Mirror, mirror on the wall.

What is it I feel when I see my reflection in the mirror? Nowadays, I feel thankful for who I have become. I breathe a huge sigh of relief knowing that I care for my well-being. I feel appreciative of myself and all that I have lived; I appreciate the difficult times I endured with what little knowledge I had about life. I feel happy when I see myself in the mirror. I am thankful for me, my life, my understanding of it. Serenity sets in; I feel it within me.

A feeling of "everything is okay" comes over me. The human in the mirror is full of emotions and ideas about life. The human in the mirror has experienced so many different situations, all the highs and lows. The human in the mirror holds everything within her, like a compass directing the course. The human in the mirror has chosen better, has chosen to comprehend the whys of life. She has chosen to win more often than not. She can see much more clearly. She can feel her way through life and be in control for once. The human in the mirror has a cup that overflows with love and joy because she chooses it to be that way. It's a cup that is filled every day from within, the overflow paving the way forward and splashing on anyone who comes close enough. The overflow is generated through self-love. Love and me: one, indeed. I love the human in the mirror and all her qualities. I respect her and admire her. I root for her every day and high five her at every chance. I am her biggest supporter and cheerleader, as she has been mine. Whether I was aware of it or not, the real me, the me who is made from love and is love... She has been there like a true ride-or-die homie.

I moved through my life without realizing that

self-love was so important, but love had its clever ways of being at my side from the very beginning of this human experience of mine.

When you really allow yourself to be real with yourself, shit starts to change. The voice inside of you starts being nicer, calmer, a little happier each day, each week. You aren't interested in all the shit you used to be, and you feel fine about that— as a matter of fact, you don't even notice until you notice, and then it's "meh." Call it what you will, but I call this change, love. Love has a beautiful way of flowing into every facet of life and making it so fuckin enjoyable. When I speak of love, I mean the feeling, the wave, the gentle breeze that sweeps over you. It's not just romantic; it's so multifaceted that it literally immerses everything in your life and elevates it to heights that just leave you speechless.

Love always sets up clever ways of making itself known, even amid painful human experiences. It speaks beautifully without saying a word.

Paw prints on my heart.

The beauty of my life, that I can see from here, is that I have been provided with just what I've needed when I've felt lost and alone. And the first of those life-sustaining gifts was a cat. God in the form of a cat.

It is said that God is in all and is all. God is the very breath of life. God is love. At the age of five, I was given my first cat. The details of how it all went down, I'm not too sure of now, but I know the experience of having been given that cat. As I sit here writing right now, I have my two male cats chilling by my side— Hansom and Prince, my associate and my silent partner, as I like to call them. Them just being in the room with me is a reminder of how much love there is for me and how much love they feel from me. It's so soothing.

That same soothing feeling I have now, I had then. I was fascinated with my cat and cared for her with all my strength. I watched her give birth many times and admired her loving ways. Each kitten was given the same affection, her actions so gentle. She never spoke a word to convey to me that she loved them. Of course, she couldn't. I just saw that her actions were loaded with love. She had so much love that she would even give me some through her purring or caressing my arms and legs at every encounter we had.

On days when I didn't feel love within my family, my cats demonstrated it instead. My little angels in disguise. I think I came to have about thirty cats at one time. Yeah, I know that sounds crazy, but we lived out in the countryside and my parents weren't going to get these cats fixed, so they had kittens every year. My parents loved that the cats caught the mice and gophers, so they allowed it for that reason, I suppose. But I know now that love was just that brilliant; it was able to trick my parents somehow!

As the years have passed, that pure love they emitted has helped me. They have remained such a catalyst to pursue unconditional love in my life. They meow and I speak the English and Spanish language, but we both feel. They remind me that love is *felt*. Yes, yes, yes. Words are lovely too, but feeling without the use of language is remarkable; something that my cats taught me.

It didn't matter how it would present itself or make itself available; love was moving around me, being active (as is its nature), allowing itself to be felt. Leaving lasting prints. Silently telling me that I was loved indeed.

CHAPTER 4

I'm everywhere you know, love.

That Special Talk Had No Words.

A few weeks before my mom passed away, I was in the Fresno airport, awaiting my flight to Seattle, listening to an audio book by Esther Hicks called, Ask and It is Given. Like with the many other books I've been led to, I was fascinated and listened attentively. The title alone reminded me of a Bible scripture in Matthew 7: "Ask, and it will be given unto you; seek and you will find; knock, and it will be opened to you." The book offered its explanation of this scripture, stating that once we ask for anything, it is a given. We believe otherwise because as we ask, we also doubt. What we are really seeking is the feeling behind that which we've asked for. And the feeling is short-lived when we allow thoughts that oppose it to take over. These new ideas were very welcomed in my mind. I added them to my memory bank as best I could. I journaled insights and pondered them. I didn't share this with anyone; it was more for me to learn and apply.

The day my mom passed was hectic and full of

emotion. I was woken up by my son and I just remember hearing the words "Guela is in the hospital" (guela is what my kids called my mom; slang for abuela). I was half asleep but hearing him say that woke my ass up quick. I had a weird feeling that this time would be different. My mother had been hospitalized on several occasions for blockage on the arterial veins of her neck. The other surgeries were nerve wracking, but I can say that I had confidence that she'd be ok. It was as if I was used to her being hospitalized and experiencing 100% recovery, so I was never too scared about the outcomes. On that day of her passing, like I said the feeling in my stomach was different; my system detected different energy in the air.

When we arrived at the hospital, the youngest of my brothers was outside. As I walked up to him, accompanied by my daughter and son, my brother could barely speak. His words "It doesn't look good this time" caused a huge lump in my throat and tears to swell up in my eyes. I don't recall saying anything, I couldn't. What the fuck was going on? Was my mom going to die today? Internally I was screaming, *Oh my gosh, oh my gosh, oh my gosh! Lord God I'm not ready for this. Please, not today! Not my mama.* As we entered the emergency room, the youngest of my older sisters greeted us. My sister had been crying, her puffy red eyes said it all. My dad and niece were sitting there, they appeared numb. My dad was staring intently at the floor and his mouth quivered as I reached out my arms to hug him. He didn't say a word. The whole environment was surreal. This couldn't really be happening! But it was and I had to ride the tumultuous wave.

My sister asked if I wanted to see our mom and of course I said yes. She warned me that mom was in a drug induced coma and didn't look good. When I walked into the room, I saw my mother with her tongue hanging out the side of her mouth. She had a large breathing tube in her mouth and nostrils. Her right arm was outstretched, hanging over the side of the bed and I immediately reached for it. I held on to her arm for dear life. I caressed her arm with my face, moving my cheek back and forth and kissed it repeatedly. All I could think was *Ama por favor no se vaya, no nos deje madresita mia (mom please don't leave, don't leave us dearest mother of mine).* The beeping sounds of all the machines and the unnatural breathing rhythm my mom was demonstrating hinted at her passing soon. I was very much in denial at this point.

I looked up with tears pouring from my eyes to see my two children equally devastated. They couldn't contain their tears. I felt so helpless. I was such a mess, but I needed to be there for my children too. I silently told my mom to forgive me for our misunderstandings and just how much I loved her. I told her that I would replicate her kind ways and loving nature, so she would live on energetically through me. This way she'd be with me all the time. And this one promise is the only promise I ever made to my mom, and I can proudly say I've honored it and continue to do so.

As a young kid my mom had always shared with me where she kept all her important documents— in an old brown vintage case, the kind you see in movies with a load of money in it. So, when it came time to gather the life insurance documents, there I was rummaging through the case. I had thumbed through it before when my mom was alive, since she also kept old photos of our family and of my paternal grandmother. I enjoyed going through it from time to time. That day again was different, though– a mix of emotions, for sure. I located the life insurance documents– oh, geesh, what a strange feeling it was. So bitter, without the sweet. I remember my uncontrollable crying. Tears falling on all her documents, creating water marks everywhere. I didn't want to believe that the time had come to use these documents for what they were intended. As I was about to close the case, I felt the urge to go through it again. And lo and behold, at the very bottom, underneath all the paperwork was a book.

The book was written in Spanish. The words on the cover were *Pide y se te Dara* by Esther Hicks. The exact book I had listened to just weeks before was now in my hand! I never saw my mom reading. I don't even recall seeing books in the house. A part of me was shocked to find it here, among her most important papers. I had no idea my mom would read such a book. And I mean no harm when I say that. It's just that we were raised Catholic and some of the ideas in the book didn't match up with anything I'd ever heard at a Catholic service. The book spoke about energy, frequencies, mind power and our connection to it all–a connection to a higher power.

I was so eager to browse through it. I saw pen marks my mom made and circled specific sentences or made notes of her own. I felt connected to her. I swear I felt like I was going a bit crazy, too. I felt so happy, so excited and so validated. I cried so much and felt so comforted. It felt like my mom wanted me to find the book. The timing was beautiful. This moment was refreshing. It was unexplainable. Words alone could not convey the sheer peace in me, the truly tranquil feeling.

A huge tidal wave of love struck me that day. I had uncovered another hidden treasure. Love had a lot more to say. The unspoken words I left my mother with that day were quickly honored back. The book was her speaking to me, silently again. Life was talking love's language, and I was sure as fuck listening. Love, the master key to unlock even more of me.

Clues Errywhere.

And that's how much love you hold. You leave clues everywhere about how awesome you are. *I do? When I do that?*

That time you cried and only you felt the hurt. Or the weekend you spent with friends that felt magical. You were present at both occasions, in which you left a piece of you there. An imprint of sorts. Even if you don't have a photo of either moment, your mind has some film that it offers to replay. Shit, sometimes it plays it even without your asking. Why could that be?

What can I learn from that part that was played by me?

Clue: a piece of evidence or information used in the detection of a crime or solving of a mystery.

Mystery: something that is difficult or impossible to understand or explain.

—That question alone is like the solving of a great mystery. And all the wonderful clues hidden and strewn out in my own history.

I, me, my Self an intriguing and captivating being. Difficult to understand or explain, we call it mystery. Every mystery has an origin. It arose from somewhere. Along the way of its creation there was movement.

That movement was stirred up by all that we knew at any given point. And at each point along the way, a piece of information was gathered. If you didn't use it then, it remains as a clue, exclusively for you.

It's exclusive due to it existing because of your own unique life. These exclusive clues are designed by you and for you. You genius You! All along you rallied dismissing the 'boos'.

You say you don't remember doing that? Look closely at yet another clue. You wouldn't be reading this, had you not silently called out to beautiful You. Love in the silent moments and in the audible too.

Hearing the lyrics of songs and singing them to myself is super fun. And it feels electrifying! Such a love fest—me singing to inner me, inner me singing to outer me, and Creator me in the other also singing to me! That kind of love energy is captivating. I feel it course through me. It is me!

Song lyrics sprinkle golden nuggets everywhere, literally. Singing along to something affirming and empowering connects all those parts within me that were previously disconnected. They click into place, because the clarity is allowing all of me to come together. Becoming one! Realizing. Clues you say. Yes. Check this out.

> ➤ Bruno Mars, 24K: "Don't fight the feeling, invite the feeling."
> ➤ Nicki Minaj/Rhianna, Fly: "I came to win, to fight. To conquer, to thrive. I came to win, to survive. To prosper, to rise. To fly, to fly. Get ready for it, Get ready for it, Get ready for it, I came to win. Get ready for it, Get ready for it, Get ready for it."
> ➤ Ariana Grande, Magic: "Redesign your brain. We gon' make some new habits. Just like magic (just like magic), just like magic (baby)."

➤ Outkast, ATLiens: "Found a way to channel my anger, now to embark. The world's a stage and everybody gets to play their part. God works in mysterious ways, so when he starts the job of speaking through us, we be so sincere with this here. No drugs or alcohol, so I can get the signal clear as day. Put my glock away. I got a stronger weapon that never runs out of ammunition, so I'm ready for war, okay."

➤ Russ, Manifest: "Movin' to the rhythm of my intuition. Anything I want I speak into Existence. That's how I'm living. That's how I'm winning."

➤ Ariana Grande, POV: "I'm getting used to receiving. Still getting good at not leaving. I'ma love you even though I'm scared (oh, scared), Learnin' to be grateful for myself (oh, oh, oh) You love my lips 'cause they say the Things we've always been afraid of I feel it startin' to subside. Learnin' to believe in what is mine."

➤ Pink Floyd, Learning to Fly: "A soul in tension that's learning to fly, condition grounded but determined to try."

➤ TI/Rhianna, Live your Life: "Look in the mirror, and keep on shinin' (shinin')
Until the game ends, 'til the clock stop We gon' post up on the top spot."

➤ Madonna/Ariana Grande, Rain on Me: "Gotta live my truth, not keep it bottled in so I don't lose my mind, baby, yeah."

➤ Taylor Swift, Shake it Off: "But I keep cruisin' Can't stop, won't stop movin' It's like I got this music in my mind saying it's gonna be alright"

Be on the lookout for those clues in the songs that light up your heart, in the songs that make you dance around. No need to tell anyone of the hunt you're on–just keep sifting through songs and paying attention. Your heart will lead the way, and the love signals your body will emit and receive as you dance and smile with glee will be clues that what you're feeling is coming from the real you.

Express Yourself.

"...we are subject to the urge of life, seeking
expression which ever drives us on to know
more, to do more and to be more."
–Wallace D. Wattles, The Science of Getting Rich

Form. Everywhere you look, there are so many different forms and structures, each distinct in one way or the other. We, human beings, along with plant and animal life, are all in existence because of that invisible life source that commonly exists in us. It's amazing to think of the shapeless, formless energy that keeps me alive and to know that I have it in common with everyone else. It's amazing just to focus on this. Nothing else.

The wonderful orchestration of this energy that keeps my body running and experiencing my physical senses is mind-blowing. It is a concept that needs to be digested slowly. A concept that will settle at its own perfect pace. When it does, it will tweak some of your thoughts. It'll begin to place thoughts in different categories; those that feel good will be encouraged, and the path to positivity will only get brighter. Eventually you'll feel it'd be silly to deny that insanely awesome energy of yours and to keep it mediocre. Life has been demonstrating what happens to forms in this world: at some point, they all will cease to have movement or life within them. The form will pass on as new forms are arriving. To me, this fact of life is like a concentrated window cleaner, providing a clarity that lasts and that allows each of us to see further ahead than ever before.

Seeing better with your inner goggles is like making easy money. It's an investment. You deposit a good thought into your current stream of thought and others will want to latch on, so you allow them to. All those positive streams will end up flowing together into a bigger body of thoughts and then onto the ocean of what is your physical life– the life you can see out here. Like I've said before, all that was played out inside, behind the curtain, will make its way onto the stage of your life.

With that being said, consider closely the script you're writing with your mind. A time comes when you're drawn onto a different path. I say "different" because it is unlike anything you have wandered onto before. Your mind begins to tell you new things. You wonder what is happening; you may even fight it by refusing to go forward. And then you feel the discomfort of not going. Where is this feeling coming from?

It's coming from the you who wants to live–the you who knows more, comprehends more, loves more, seeks more, is more. Everywhere you go, the pull is there. At every turn there's a message you can't ignore. You receive something like love notes from all over the place; you feel them.

I accept the idea that we are all connected by something called life, Source, Creator, God. The belief that we all come from One and return to One is liberating. It is a mindset that welcomes freedom that is so refreshing and renewing. Spirit energy comes in unlimited forms, all from One source, all playing various roles.

Plato's Theory of Recollection affirms that the soul of the human being is immortal and knows the universal truth before entering the body. This is why humans gradually remember what the soul already knows when it is formed. After the soul inhabits the human body, its knowledge is buried in the depths of being and then gradually remembered during encounters with physical realities (objects/forms) of the sensual world. According to Plato, all knowledge is found in the soul of the human being; but the human being is only able to recall it through contact with copies or reflections of forms or ideas. We're here to mix it up, to benefit one another, and to benefit from one another. We're sparks of life illuminating paths and ready to remember what living feels like.

Therefore, from within me, I now place things beautifully, from a place of memory. I jump for joy now with ideas that shine brightly. I just sit back and admire the origin of their wonderful creation, of their energy; I let myself soak in what "together" feels like. The times when I've felt weird have been when I've felt most like myself—when I've felt like the ideal me. Doing what came naturally to me, despite what others thought of it... I wish I'd let that be my guiding light. The light wasn't far away though, as it was reflected back to me in others. The light of love finds its way, because it is the way.

What a beautiful place to be: in love with myself, and in love with my life. Try slowing down a bit and looking inside. What do you see and feel? This is the core of your creating. You may not have thought so, but a careful exploration and understanding of what you have lived through will show you that you created it all. It isn't pleasant to the ears to hear that we have created good and bad days, as we call them. But in knowing that we play a part, we give ourselves some power back, because that means we're gonna' get involved now. Breathe a huge sigh of relief now, because you are now taking ownership of yourself.

Say: "Move aside old shell and thank you for your service to me and the whole. I now release you with love and gratitude. On to put on a new shell I go!" A new normal is here; love has taken its rightful place, because I—and you—have chosen it so!

I am always home, and I love it here now.

Taking the inward journey has its unique way of doing things. It's spring cleaning, right before you blossom.

I feel more and more at home. I have—and I am— a home all to my own. Here, I dance with wisdom, unlimited power, love, serenity and joy. I build, I tear down, all for the better. Always refining, always shining. I weather the emotional storms, but my path is never covered up or erased. My path, the golden path for me, is always there just as the sun is each day. It's a guarantee.

The whole feel of my life is different now. The fact that I did change, in a way that freed me, is fucking awesome. And the fact that I chose to do it, that I was aware of what I was doing for myself, is even better.

As crazy and messy as life seems and as crazy and

messy as we feel sometimes, it really is comforting to know that life can be fun. Life is just being life, everything under the sun is going on, has been going on and will continue to do so long after my passing. With that in mind, I know that the inward journey, the looking back, the extracting, the learning and the making peace with it all, is liberating. Allow yourself a chance to become who you are. Understanding how you work and why you work that way is one of the most beautiful gifts we can give ourselves.

When we care for our individuality, we literally cause a ripple effect that stretches into days ahead of us. All the care and affection we hold for ourselves gathers momentum. However life calls out to you, give yourself the opportunity to hear it out. Check the love odometer— that always helps. Be willing to be moldable and open to mental upgrades. Feel everything out. Let your gut— your intuition— speak to you. Sit back and listen to the conversations within yourself. Start new conversations of celebration and happiness. Be willing to tear down the old constructs that aren't really yours.

You feel for a reason, so let those feelings help guide you in every way, every day. The script, life with its new days, is a book of blank pages awaiting your direction. A small turn, a nudge here or there from within, can make all the difference. This is a journey where the map is created by you and open to changes. In fact, changes are welcome— so move as you were meant to: as unique and beautiful you.

Printed in the United States
by Baker & Taylor Publisher Services